The Cliff Walk

The Cliff Walk

A Memoir of a Job Lost and a Life Found

DON J. SNYDER

LITTLE, BROWN AND COMPANY

Boston New York Toronto London

First Edition

The author is grateful for permission to include the following previously copyrighted material: Excerpt from *Death of a Salesman* by Arthur Miller. Copyright 1949, renewed © 1977 by Arthur Miller. Reprinted by permission of Viking Penguin, a division of Penguin Books, USA Inc.

Library of Congress Cataloging-in-Publication Data

Snyder, Don J.
    The cliff walk : a memoir of a job lost and a life found / Don J.
Snyder. — 1st ed.
        p.   cm.
      ISBN 0-316-80308-1
      1. Snyder, Don J.   2. Downsizing of organizations — United States —
Case studies.   3. College teachers — Dismissal of — United States —
Case studies.   4. Job security — United States — Case studies.
5. Career changes — United States — Case studies.   6. Life change
events — United States — Case studies.   7. College teachers — United
States — Biography.   I. Title.
HF5549.5.D55S628   1997
331.13 — dc21
[B]   96-51163

10 9 8 7 6 5 4 3 2 1

Published simultaneously in Canada by Little, Brown & Company (Canada) Limited

Printed in the United States of America

For Nell

The Cliff Walk

Prologue

I made my confession to a rich woman this week. It followed a long run of terrible luck that she happened to come upon me just as I was breaking into the Winslow Homer cottage, where I'd been hired to do some painting. I had misplaced the owner's keys and was prying open a porch door when she came crashing through the bushes like a fullback. "I'm looking for a man to fix my windows!" she bellowed. She was breathing hard and stood with her feet planted wide apart.

I asked what was wrong with her windows and she said some of them wouldn't go up and some of them went up but didn't stay up. She didn't think it was going to be a big job. I've heard this before. Most of these ancient wood and shingle cottages on the Maine coast are crumbling beneath the surface, brutalized by decades of North Atlantic winters. You start out to put a quick coat of paint on one short board below the eaves, you get up there and find the board is soggy, you pull it off and the ends of the roof rafters crumble like old paper, and then you're left rebuilding the house and trying to explain to someone with a year-round tan why a fifty-dollar paint job is going to cost thousands.

We talked about the money right up front because I have learned that many rich people still believe that only their doctors, lawyers, and accountants deserve a living wage. "I charge fifteen dollars an hour," I told her.

"That's fine," she said.

"Well, I'll come have a look," I said.

At the end of the day I followed her through the grape arbor. She walked at a good clip, dressed in layers of white and topped off with a white lace shawl that caught her tangled silver hair and gave her the appearance of one of Tennessee Williams's aimless women.

It was early spring and the couches in her house still lay under white sheets like cadavers. The rooms were enormous, with handsome wood walls of oak and walnut, stone fireplaces, and stamped tin ceilings. Everything shimmered in a riot of sunlight from the lovely floor-to-ceiling windows. I had been in a number of these cottages in the year since I began earning my living as a painter. The rich women hired me because I did a good job, taking the time to sand off all the old paint, and because I cleaned up after myself and didn't show up with a boom box to keep me company.

Usually I am cautious about saying much to the summer people because it is easy to hear yourself turning into a character in a cocktail party narrative back home in St. Louis or Chicago: "*Oh, I've got this carpenter in Maine, he's an absolute classic!*" But it was different this time. She told me that she had happened to be watching the time my four kids came by and I let them each take a turn painting the Homer cottage. "I could tell right away that those are four happy children," she said. This made me feel comfortable enough to explain how, lately, I had been trying to teach myself to look up and behold them. Just the other night, I said, we had all been hurrying to get to a fifth grade concert. I was in the kitchen cleaning up after dinner to the rhythm of the radio news, doing my compulsive little nightly dance with the sponge and dish towel — if the news is particularly bad I polish the copper bottoms of the pots — when I glanced into the next room and saw my world of beauty and surprise. There was our three-year-old in her Lion King undies, white ruffled socks, and black patent leather shoes, all her ribs exposed as she stretched her arms up high so her ten-year-old sister could drop the white and blue sailor dress over her head (HOLD STILL, CARA!) while her nine-year-old sister tied pink ribbons in her pigtails (STOP JUMPING UP AND DOWN, CARA!) and her seven-year-old brother put Band-Aids on her knees as a result of her having spent the day trying to ride a two-wheeler (DON'T MOVE, CARA!).

"It made me think of them decorating the Christmas tree," I told her. "There it is in front of you, what you work for, and the reason you live. I happened to look up at the right moment or I would have missed it." My little story didn't seem to register with her at first, she just kept on walking out ahead of me. But at the bottom of the stairs she stopped and turned to face me, and told me that I was a lucky man, that her own father had been very handy but he'd never had the patience to teach her how to do anything. "So now I'm helpless," she said without a trace of self-pity. "Can't even make my own windows stay up."

The first two days I worked alone in her house while she disappeared into the rest of her life. I can never stop myself from snooping around these amazing cottages, taking inventory and trying to piece together a picture of how rich people live. You almost always find trophies from golf and tennis tournaments, and a little glass panel of bells and wires that once summoned the hired help to different rooms. And very often one of the old vibrating machines people once used to reduce fat. Walking through the empty rooms of her house, it didn't take long to figure out that this had been her father's house and that he had run the show with an iron hand. There were paintings of him in different rooms that showed him distant and glowering. His daughter had preserved his study and his working desk with such meticulous care that I thought of the room across the street from Ford's Theatre where Lincoln had died. In fact I began to see her less as a resident of the house than as a curator of a museum. Most telling were the family photographs that depicted her as a lovely little girl with a winsome smile that slowly vanished from successive photographs as her father appeared with different women at his side.

I had uncovered a lot of her history by the time she returned, and as the days went by we began to spend a little time before I left each afternoon just sitting and talking on what she called "the wicker porch," where you could hear English bicycles ticking like Geiger counters beyond the tall hedges, and off in the distance the dull concussion of tennis balls on the clay courts. One afternoon she told me that her father had been married five times and that each of his wives, as part of their divorce, had been paid off with a piece of this house. With all their children and grandchildren, she was allowed one week a year here. "I open up the place and then clear out right after Memorial Day weekend," she said. "Ahead of the black flies."

I admired her equanimity, and I told her that she reminded me of my wife. "She's a woman who takes things in stride and can handle anything," I said. "All she really asks of her husband is that he doesn't plague her."

She laughed hard at this.

My last day she wrote me out a check, and as she handed it to me told me again how lucky I was to have such a beautiful wife and children. I told her the truth about myself then: that like a lot of people in this country I had lost my job and all my money and everything else that I'd always believed added up to the promise of a secure life. How I'd had things my own way for so long that when this happened I spent most of two years feeling sorry for myself and looking for somebody to blame. How I took solace from news reports about how hard life had become in America, until I realized that life had always been hard for a lot of people, people I thought I was better than, and that the only thing that had changed was that bad things were finally starting to happen to people like me who had it so good for so long. I told her that the whole time I was putting my family through hard times I knew what was the best thing to do for them and what was the worst thing, and I always chose the worst thing because it was easier.

I didn't tell her that I'd spent so many years as a bullshitter that I got to the point where I could lie about anything. I don't mean just the harmless lies that we tell each other, I mean the lies we tell ourselves. For me these lies went way back to old autumn afternoons when I was a golden boy who came out of the football locker room into the cold light and crossed the parking lot in my spiked shoes, helmet on or cocked under one arm. On my way to the practice field I passed the high school hoods sitting on the steps out behind the wood shop, hunched over their cigarettes, watching me with a bored, superior look. They had nothing but disdain for guys like me, knowing I believed things about myself that they already knew were not true. I looked down on them with their go-to-hell sunglasses and their shit-kicker boots, and I left them behind on my way to an exceptional life.

Their names are still real to me. Percy Sergeant. Wayne Lavasseur. Paul Gaudette. And now I think of them as survivors of some kind of night journey that I never believed was out there for me. I remember how desperately I had always wanted to dance with America and how I had always wanted to believe that I could hear the band starting up in the distance for me, and how those boys outside the wood shop had already taken America by the hand and disappeared with her down Flamingo Lane. We all came of age when America was under a new coat of paint, in the midst of her magic trick when she could still pull the rabbit out of the hat. Lately, the magician has slowed down and you can see the little trap doors and hinges in her act. Maybe this accounts for why the disillusionment is spreading into the middle class, not because the disillusionment is rising but because people like me are finally falling. Falling hard.

That last day in her cottage I told her I could show her how to fix her windows in case one of them ever broke again. She looked into my eyes. It was a small thing but it pleased her. She took the time to put on an apron first, and then we climbed the stairs to the third floor. She chose a window with pencil marks and small print on the edge of one of the trim boards. It was where her mother had measured her from summer to summer, across the good days, I suppose, before her father showed her how hard life could be. There was a beautiful light in her eyes when she discovered the simplicity of the window's mechanism: a length of rope with one end attached to an iron weight and the other slotted in the window frame. "I never would have guessed," she exclaimed. I pointed out that the fixtures were made of solid bronze, like the fittings on fine ships, and that the joints had been done by hand. I stood there watching her and thinking how safe she must have felt in this house before the trouble began. Suddenly I saw her as a little girl, and then it was like she was one of *my* daughters. I still don't know if I was seeing them in her, or her in them. When I left she was standing in the late-afternoon light with a hammer in her hand.

1

When word started getting around the university that I'd been fired, a student came up to me after class one morning and gave me the lay of the land. He was a smart kid, sweet too. He said he was sorry first, then he let me have it. "Man, not another baby boomer out of work," he said, shaking his head. "Every time one of you guys loses his real job you take the crap jobs at Blockbuster and the mall so I can't even pick up summer work."

I dismissed this comment. Things had gone so well for me for so long that I didn't see I was standing right next to him on a dividing line between how you imagine your life will turn out and how it actually does. After spending my whole grown-up life shaking hands, making promises, and smiling at the right people in order to be liked and to get ahead, to stay ahead and never slip, I was a man who had forgotten how lucky he was.

It was early March of 1992, I was forty-one, married, with

three children under seven years old and a fourth due in June. We were living an unhurried life in upstate New York, in a small town in a big house on easy street where we paid our way each month without much sweat.

This was pretty much the same safe and privileged life I had known from the time I left behind the rattrap apartments of my childhood in Bangor, Maine, for a classy private college on a football scholarship and then graduate school on a big fat fellowship I don't remember even being grateful for. I was in the passing lane, leaving behind my uncles, grandfathers, and cousins who lived out their lives as low-wage, no-ambition, Lawrence Welk on Saturday nights, two weeks off a year, classic American working stiffs. They were nice enough guys but guys who were going nowhere. As soon as I was old enough to see how the world worked I began working hard to get enough velocity in my own life to escape theirs like a man fleeing a fire.

I never looked back. I went from one promising job to the next. Even when I had a good job I was always looking for a better one, and sometimes I would take job interviews just for the chance to see what I was worth to a stranger and to listen to him tell me how marvelous I was. I had quit a good job at the University of Maine, where I was completely happy, to take a job in the Department of English at Colgate University for more money than the combined income of both of my uncles when they retired. At the time there was that goofy commercial on television where a handsome Irishman goes dashing across an impossibly green field, smiling like a politician because he's so happy with his new deodorant soap. It could have been filmed on the Colgate University campus, where the lawns and the playing fields were as lush and green as Ireland when we arrived in late-August 1989. My students affectionately called the place Camp Colgate and the

Colgate Country Club, and told me that they had chosen this over other schools because of the university's ski slopes, which I could see from my office window, or the squash courts and beautiful indoor tennis courts, or the award-winning eighteen-hole golf course and the trap-shooting range that were a short bike ride from campus, or because the university was ranked academically among the top twenty in the country for getting students into law school, or because Colgate had been celebrated as one of the nation's best party schools, based upon its per capita consumption of alcohol.

My own reason for choosing Colgate was no more substantial: it was right up there with the Ivy League schools, maybe not quite an Ivy League school, but definitely just one step, one job away. There was also a long list of irresistible perks that included several thousand dollars to order any books I wished for the library; a retreat on Lake Saranac where we could spend weekends as a family and have our meals prepared for us; a low-interest loan for the purchase of a house in town a few blocks from campus; a gift of three grand for a summer project, plus paid student research assistants if I needed them; generous health, dental, and life insurance plans; a marvelous retirement pension plan that would multiply like cells dividing; free tuition for my wife to take courses toward her master's in education and for my four children to attend any college in America; a discount in the campus bookstore; a new Macintosh computer system; a paid sabbatical leave after three years of teaching; and most of all, time. Five weeks off at Christmas, ten days off during spring break, three months in the summer. This amounted to roughly eighteen weeks of paid vacation per year. Plus an additional ten weeks if you added up my two free days each work week of the academic year.

It was a dream. My full teaching load was nine hours a week in the classroom first semester, six the second. There had never been a violent crime in town. We bought a six-bedroom house on a tree-lined street a few blocks from campus and the elementary school. In contrast to the nonacademic residents of town, most of whom earned little more than the minimum wage, my faculty salary enabled us to live like royalty, and Colleen was able to fulfill her long-standing desire to stay at home with our children.

That first winter it snowed every day in December but two, and the campus was transformed into a wonderland. We pulled the kids all over town on their sleds, and got them up on skis. Colleen taught them her fine technique for making angels in the snow. Once when I turned my head from a department meeting on the third floor of Lawrence Hall to glance out the window, I saw my whole family down in the quad putting the finishing touches on a giant snowman. It made me feel that our life was charmed.

I remember the nights best. They were so magnificently cold and bright that Colleen and I often stood outside looking up at the stars before we went to bed. The only tension between us in those days was the result of my wife's honesty. A true Maine woman, she felt no need to try and impress anyone. I was in the faculty lounge schmoozing the feminists in the department one morning when Colleen appeared with the kids. They got to talking and when one of my colleagues related how she had gone straight back to work after her baby was born because she didn't feature spending her days at home changing diapers, Colleen coolly announced that on the worst days there were maybe ten diapers and each took no longer than a minute and a half to change. The feminists looked at her like she was quaint or exotic, and when we were alone I cautioned Colleen that someday I might need letters of recommendation from these women in order to grab a better job at a much better school.

The best part about the job by far was my students. They were so pleasant and eager to please that I went the extra mile, taking on more of them as my advisees than anyone else in the department, inviting them to our house for dinner and movies, and teaching literature with a no-holds-barred passion that made my classes some of the most popular on campus. That wasn't hard, really, because these were the days in academia when most professors droned on about preposterous literary theories while their students fought bravely against sleep. I was well paid for my efforts and nominated every spring for "Professor of the Year" by the Student Honor Society, which sent me beautiful letters extolling my devotion to bringing literature to life for students.

In fact I received another one of those letters in March of 1992, my third year, the same day the dean of faculty wrote to inform me that I was being fired.

The terms of my dismissal were as fair as anyone could ask for: I would be allowed to finish the rest of my third year and to return for a fourth with a pay raise, full benefits, and an additional stipend of three thousand dollars if I wished to serve as advisor to the debate club. Meanwhile the dean would recommend me highly to other universities, with an official letter that said I was being dismissed simply because the English department was already top-heavy with tenured professors.

In all the jobs I had held across the years, from the first, picking vegetables when I was thirteen, I had never been fired. My first reaction was that some mistake had been made. *They got the wrong guy.* They don't know that Colleen has just finished making curtains for the house and painting the kids' rooms and we've just drained our savings account of its last nine thousand dollars to replace the cast iron pipes with copper and to strip the basement of asbestos. *They got the wrong guy.* They don't know that we've got a new baby coming, and that my father has a brain tumor that is taking over his life.

I sat on our back porch and read the letter several times before I walked to campus, climbed the hill to the dean of faculty's office, and waited there until he could see me. I had enough self-confidence then — or maybe it was arrogance or just a long history of successes — to think that I would be able to fix things. I'd say the perfect thing. I'd tell him about all my achievements. I'd make the right impression and the decision would be recanted. It would be like nothing had ever happened.

I watched the secretaries answering telephones and typing into their computers. Okay, I thought, this is what I'm going to do, I'm going to explain very calmly to the Dean that I'm the only professor in the English department who teaches a freshman seminar, the only one who teaches an upper-level general education course every term, the only one who volunteers to teach multiple sections of the required survey course, and that no one has taken on more advisees or sponsored more independent studies than I have. The dean doesn't know me personally so I have to make him see *who I am*. With three published books to my credit, a stunning graduate school record, and letters of generous praise in my dossier, all I have to do is press the pedal down a little harder.

He was gracious and in a hurry. While he was promising that he would write me glorious letters saying how I was loved by my students and respected by my colleagues, I was watching him glance at the big clock on the wall, and I was thinking, Wait a second, pal, you're not going to give me the bum's rush here. We're going to take a long time, maybe the rest of the afternoon, because I've got a lot of wonderful things to tell you about myself and about the work I've done here while you were playing computer golf in your office.

I laid it out for him, but I could tell by the way his smile never changed that I was already floating off his screen. I heard my voice climbing a little too high as I explained to him that my father was ill and that we had a new baby coming. When at last he put his hand out for me to shake, I was short of breath.

His pasted-on smile. My embarrassment. "I'm sorry," he said, showing me to the door.

That night I read *The Littlest Angel* to Nell and Erin at bedtime. When they conked out I sat down on the floor by their nightlight and tried to figure out the finances of losing my job. With monthly expenses of just over two thousand dollars, I figured that we would be able to save around $140 dollars each month from my remaining paychecks. That was seventeen monthly paychecks until I would be cut off on August 1, 1993. Two thousand three hundred eighty dollars. But before my last check I would have to reimburse Colgate the five thousand dollars they had loaned me for a down payment on the house. So, aside from whatever it was going to cost to move, we were going to be short by almost three thousand.

I waited until Colleen was asleep that night and then I walked from room to room with a flashlight, taking inventory of our possessions and deciding what we could sell and for how much. The washer and dryer were worth four hundred. How Colleen had loved having a proper laundry room, with its wide window taking in the afternoon sun. She folded laundry every day at the long low shelf below this window, though I couldn't remember ever seeing her do it. In the dining room there was the table I had built out of rough boards. It was worth maybe twenty bucks now that it was permanently stained from the kids doing their oil paintings there with Colleen. In the playroom another table worth another twenty bucks. I shined the flashlight up at a corner of the ceiling that I had patched with sheetrock; I had done dozens of jobs like that in the house; there wasn't any job I wouldn't tackle so long as it fit my one criterion — I had to be able to begin the job and complete it in a single day because, after all, I was a busy man with more important things to do. Along the windowsills Colleen had lined up the seedlings she was growing with the kids in anticipation of a garden by summer. I knelt down and read the little name tags of each plant scrawled in the girls' handwriting. I thought how long it must have taken them to write the names, making mistakes, erasing, starting over again, their mother waiting patiently and encouraging them until the names were right. In the kitchen I examined the refrigerator, moving aside the magnetic letters and checking for scratches. Two hundred dollars, maybe. In the guest room was a bureau made of cherry that had to be worth four hundred. It had belonged to my father when he was a young man, and Colleen had already identified it as more than a piece of furniture; it was something she wanted to pass on to our children. In the living room there were two couches, each worth a hundred and fifty. Two wing chairs that had to be worth at least seventy-five. The one near the woodstove was where Colleen spent a winter breast-feeding Jack. I saw her unbuttoning her blouse for him and cupping his blond head in one hand while she fed him. Upstairs she was in each room, in the mobiles swaying above the kids' beds, and the needlepoint murals hanging on the walls, and the stenciled bureaus. I followed the bright shaft of light through the darkness, feeling more and more like a burglar, a stranger in this house. Colleen and the kids had *lived* in these rooms that I had merely passed through.

I figured somewhere around fourteen hundred. And maybe if we lived very carefully we could cut our monthly miscellaneous expenses from four hundred to two hundred. That would mean another $3,400. So, after repaying Colgate the five thousand, we might have two thousand left by the time I was cut off.

The next day I went to the human resources office and found out that I could cash in my pension for $16,800, minus $3,200 in tax penalties. I added this amount of $13,600 to our projected savings of $2,000: $15,600. It didn't look bad at all. I had seventeen more months on Colgate's payroll, and by the last month we would have $15,600 in an emergency fund. Then I would begin a new job with a new monthly income kicking in. So as long as we could sell our house for as much as we'd paid for it, there was really nothing to worry about.

But when it came to telling Colleen that I had been fired, I never could seem to find the right time, or the right room in our house. There was always her with her lovely pregnant belly and her faith in me, and then there was me with my pink slip.

The night I finally told her, it was good and cold, cold enough to skate on the backyard rink I had built. When I went upstairs to our bedroom, I found Colleen asleep with a book in her hand. I knelt down and leaned close enough to her face to feel her breath. In the late stages of her pregnancies I used to love to lift up her nightgown while she slept and watch the baby rolling around in her belly. Tonight each time the baby moved, Colleen's eyelids fluttered. I sat there for a long time before I kissed her cheek to awaken her.

"Did someone throw up?" she asked me.

"Let's go skating," I said.

"What time is it?"

"Late," I said. "Middle of the night."

She closed her eyes and waved goodbye to me.

"I'll make hot chocolate?"

She sighed.

"If I carry you downstairs, will you skate with me?"

"If you try to carry me downstairs, you'll never skate again," she said.

By the time we reached the ice I was lost in her pretty face just as I had been the first time I saw her ten years before. Under starlight we did our Olympic skit of the two Russian ice dancers, Nikita and Vladimir, drunk on vodka, that always made the kids laugh. I twirled her around in the cone of white light from the spotlight. I was looking at her and feeling her presence so deep inside me it was as if there were no space between where I ended and she began. What I liked best about moments like this was how different we seemed from the rest of humanity. Everyone else in the world was asleep in their boring lives, their clothes laid out on a chair for the next day, which would not distinguish itself from the day before. Not us. We were up and on the move.

"Here's the news, beautiful," I finally said. "I got fired."

She turned and faced me and asked if I was telling her the truth. When I heard the disappointment in her voice it surprised me because across the years *she* had been the adventurous one in our marriage, right from the start, when we eloped in England and snuck into a first class train compartment and made love beneath our overcoats. She had always loved new places. In 1987, when we had saved a little money for a down payment on a house, she decided we should use it to go to Ireland for the winter. We had a newborn baby and an eighteen-month-old and we were

19

flying across the Atlantic in the dark of night, still undecided whether we would get off the plane in Shannon or Dublin.

I felt her pull her hand out of mine. The spell was broken and she glided away from me. "Now we'll be free to try out for the winter Olympics," I called to her.

At first she didn't say anything. Then she skated back and told me how her father had been laid off once when she was a little girl; he was so ashamed he pretended to go to work each day, and for a couple of months he fooled the family.

"Your father's like all the men I grew up around," I told her. "To them, all the great enterprises of life — political elections, religion, even love itself — had no meaning unless they were holding down a job."

She turned away and skated back into the darkness. I was wondering if she was going to mark this as the first bad thing that had happened to us in the ten years since we'd met, years she had spent happily with her healthy, smiling babies in tow, while the screaming siren in the dead of night was always for someone else.

"Who needs this place?" I called to her. I skated to her side and took her hand again. I told her there was plenty of time for me to find another job. I pulled her close. "Where do you want to go next?" I asked. She rested her head on my shoulder and didn't say anything. I pressed my face against her hair and looked up through the branches of a tree at a constellation of stars that I couldn't name. I asked her which one it was and she told me. Colleen had tried hard to get me to pay attention to such things, to learn the types of flowers and trees in the places where we had lived together so I could teach our children. I had always heard her and never complied with her efforts to get me to live in the present tense, the way small children do, rather than how I had always lived, inside my vast intentions and vague ideas, which, to her, were only dull abstractions when set alongside something as fine as the starlight above us. I don't know. Blame it on my escape velocity, I guess. I was moving too fast to pay much attention.

"I know it's only a job to you," she said thoughtfully.

Then I knew what it was — for me this place was just another stop on the long arc of achievement and acquisition, but Colleen had made a home here.

I told her everything would be all right. "I'm not worried at all," I said.

"It's just that the kids are so happy here," she said. She looked back at our house. "Erin and Nell in their school. Jack learned to walk here . . . and with the new baby coming . . . I don't know, I guess I just didn't want to have to think about moving."

"We don't have to think about it for a whole year," I told her again.

"And I thought you were happy here too," she said softly. "You seemed happy."

"I have been happy," I said. "And I'll be happy someplace else. But that part is way down the road. You don't have to think about it now."

"I'll think about it every day," she said. And this, I recognize now, was the difference between us; I would put my head down and plow right through the next year and then move on without ever looking back even to write a letter to anyone I'd known here. But from now on, each time Colleen was with her friends she would think about having to leave them.

When she reached the porch I called to her. "What I meant is, it's no big deal, Colleen. I lost a job, that's all. I'll find a better one."

When she opened the back door, light from the kitchen fell onto the snowbanks. I watched her stop in the doorway and I thought she was going to wait there for me or tell me to come up to bed. But instead, she stood with her head down for just a moment in the box of yellow light and then went inside and closed the door.

Recalling that night, I see her hesitating there in the lighted doorway of the house where she would wake in the night to feed the new baby, sitting at the front windows and looking across the darkened rooftops of houses where people she cared about lived.

I stayed outside and skated by myself for a while. Maybe some people lay awake at night taking stock of themselves, measuring the sum of what they possess in this world, of all that they have worked hard to attain and how easily they might lose it. Not me. Not then, anyway.

2

Cara was born in June. She was a real beauty, and nothing else mattered for a while as we were all cast into the blissful trance that a newborn baby bestows upon a family. She gazed at us with clear, knowing eyes, and I, like some napping navy commander who thinks the torpedo that just ripped off the bow of his ship was only a passing school of tuna, told myself that being one of the millions of Americans to be laid off, passed over, downsized, or just plain screwed out of a job was only a temporary setback. "Wow, four kids under seven," one of my more practical colleagues said to me. To which I gave my stock response: "We're still hoping for a set of twins."

I could afford to be smug; because Colgate had given me another year of employment, I had the whole summer, fall, and winter and then another spring and summer in which to find a new job. I was sure that it would be a piece of cake.

In July I put our house up for sale as casually as if it were a motel we'd been staying in, and I left it to Colleen to persuade our children that leaving behind the only school they had ever known and friends they were old enough to miss was no big deal. Erin, our oldest, turned seven in September. We had a small party for her, and when everyone had gone home and Colleen was upstairs putting the other kids to bed I lay on the living room floor with Erin and described for her how much more beautiful the next town we lived in would be and how much bigger our next house would be. "But I like *this* house, Daddy," she said sadly.

"Oh yes, I know *you do,* sweetheart," I said. "But just wait until you *see* the next house."

She perked up a little and looked into my eyes and said, "You already know what it looks like?"

"Well," I improvised, "not really."

"How do you know then? How do you know it will be nicer than my house now?"

"Because," I said, "Daddy didn't really have a great job here, not nearly as great as his new job will be."

By then I had begun applying for new, and I believed unfailingly, *better,* jobs. Job openings for college professors are listed in the professional journals, and this was important to me because it meant that I didn't have to read the pedestrian help wanted pages in newspapers the way I had seen my father doing when I was growing up. By the late fall of that year twenty-three openings in my field had been announced. I threw my hat into the ring for all of them, though I considered all but three or four beneath me.

We had a good last year at the university. Like anyone who has ever taught young people at any level I had experienced from time to time an extraordinary feeling of gratitude when, working with a student, something would click and suddenly I felt certain that fate was at work. Fate had sorted through our random flights across the planet so that our paths would cross at the precise moment in time when the student's life required just a nudge in order to turn toward fulfillment. It's a custodial thing—the housekeeper, while draping her coat over the back of a kitchen chair, casually turns the potted plant toward the light; it's just a half turn and she does it without a thought in her head, but it then enables the plant to flourish. This is the reason, I believe, that certain professions are still referred to as callings, and this calling, which for me had always been just a faint rustling in the grass, began, in my last months at Colgate, to turn to a steady breeze.

Dan, a big tough football player with better things to do than study, came down the university ski slope backwards on a cafeteria tray at two in the morning and cracked his head open like a watermelon on one of the iron ski lift stanchions. He was not expected to live, but after he spent two months in the hospital his father called me and said Dan had been asking about me, and would I be able to come see him, and (this was the astonishing part) would I bring the novel *Revolutionary Road* by Richard Yates that I had been telling him he should read. Fate, I thought.

Paul, who dreamed only of being a filmmaker, had somehow pissed off the professors in the art department whose letters of recommendation would have carried great weight on his application to graduate film school. He was my advisee and I persuaded him not to be discouraged and to apply to the best film school in the country, UCLA. I'd never had a single student accepted there, but I felt strangely *called* to this student and to this letter of recommendation and I proceeded to work on it for two weeks, crafting each paragraph with absolute care. After he was accepted his parents came to town to thank me. We were having dinner when his father leaned across the table and told me that Colgate had made a terrible mistake letting me go. "That's the way it is so often in this world," he said. "Think of it like this. Pearls before swine. Pearls before swine."

Exactly, I told myself. *Pearls before swine.* I liked the sound of this, I liked the taste of defiance in my mouth. I liked the way it got me off the hook for losing my job and left me feeling that my colleagues were a little ways below me, poor unimaginative people stuck where they were. I was different, I was only passing through on my way to someplace where the colors were brighter.

And so I turned my final months at Colgate into acts of subversion and revenge. Late one afternoon I stopped by the office of the department chair to announce to her that we were missing the boat terribly because we taught our students as if they were going to grow up and become academic nerds like ourselves instead of real people who would inhabit the real world where literature, and especially poetry, could bring them insight and comfort and redemption from life's sadness. "It's murder," I said, dragging her by the arm down the corridor to look at a student association poster that had been hung above the stairwell at the beginning of final exams: SELL YOUR BOOKS BACK TO THE USED BOOK STORE THE MINUTE YOUR LAST EXAM IS OVER AND JOIN US IN THE PUB!!!

"You see what we're up against," I said with conviction.

There are many good people in universities, and she was one of them. She stood there pleasantly when I told her that we were accomplices in the murder of literature.

Then came a colleague's Valentine's Day party, when, as I was opening the refrigerator to get a can of beer, I heard some professors talking about how overworked they were. "I know a nurse who makes more money than I do," one of them complained. I wasn't in the mood for a party anyway. Earlier in the day one of my favorite students had shown me an exam he'd just taken. On the top of the page was the professor's name and then the date. February 1982. He'd been using the same exam for more than ten years. "First I just shook my head and laughed," the student said to me. "Then when I started thinking about how hard my father works to put me through this place, I got mad."

I went up to the professors. "I've never known a professor who works as hard as a nurse," I said. One of them, a nice guy with the disheveled look of a man just shot out of a cannon, tried to tell me he put in eighty hours a week. "That's a lot of hours," I said. "How many hours are you in class each week?"

"Six," he said.

"Six," I said. "Office hours?"

"Three," he said.

"Three," I said. "That's nine hours. You've got seventy-one hours to go." I watched the other two people walk away from us. "And as for nurses," I said to him through a cloud of smoke as he was trying to respond. I thought I was going to enjoy making him squirm, but as I watched him I began to feel sorry for him. "Never mind," I said.

In bed that night, after I'd defended my position to Colleen, she said quietly, "These are just people who go to work every day and do the best they can. What were you trying to prove?"

"Nothing, nothing at all," I said. "I mean, he's just been promoted and I've been dumped, so I don't know what I'm talking about. Right?"

Colleen just looked at me. "I don't know what to say to you, but you're getting angrier," she said. "This whole last year, ever since you were let go, you've been getting angrier, and I'm worried about you."

I should have let it go, but I was becoming hooked on the

narcotic of defiance, and so it was hard to give anyone else the last word. "While we're talking about it," I said, "I've been thinking that when we go back to Maine we shouldn't rent a house in your parents' neighborhood."

We had decided by then that when we left Colgate we would return home, and we had spoken often about trying to find a house near Colleen's folks. We had both spoken cheerfully to our children about this new proximity to their grandparents and now, suddenly, I couldn't imagine ever spending a single day there.

"Why?" Colleen asked.

I thought for a second or two and then told her that I wanted to live near the ocean.

"So does everyone else who comes to Maine for the summer," she said. "It would be way too expensive."

"Yeah, well," I said, "I think we deserve it." At that moment I was short of breath over the dismal possibility of living in a working-class neighborhood without a job that was exalted enough to distinguish me clearly from my neighbors. How would I convince these neighbors, and myself, that I was still moving forward? God, what if there were backyard barbeques and people dropping by unexpectedly to catch me at home on working days? How would I persuade these neighbors that I was only pausing on my way to some great new shining chance?

Out of the blue several of my students organized a petition drive that spring, demanding that I be rehired. Better than three hundred students placed their signatures on the petition and presented it to the university president. Soon signs began appearing at the student center and the bookstore, and after the school newspaper reported that a recent graduate had returned his prestigious literature award in protest of my firing, large bedsheet banners hung from the dormitory windows. I pretended not to notice, and whenever students asked me about my plans I explained that we were happy to be leaving town. "We're going home to Maine," I would say. On one warm spring night when Cara woke up hungry I fixed a bottle of milk for her and carried her in my arms on a walk across campus. Her eyes were wide open as we passed beneath the great bending willow trees. You do silly things with little babies sometimes, and that night I held her up so she could see my name emblazoned on the bedsheets across the sides of the dormitories. Life being as crazy as it is in these last days of the twentieth century, I suppose the only way a person can be sure he's losing his balance is if he starts to think of himself as a character in a Hollywood movie. I had this epic scene in mind from the television miniseries *Roots* where the father holds his newborn baby up to the stars and pronounces his place in the world. Suddenly I was deeply moved by what the students had done on my behalf, and by the time we returned home and I put my daughter back to bed I had decided that I wanted to do something to show my appreciation.

And what better thing, I decided, than to leave them with the gift of literature. I mean the majesty of literature. The pure power it conveys when it isn't waterlogged by scholars' literary theories and professors' canned lectures.

I came up with the idea of having the makeup person in the theater department turn me into Walt Whitman. It was a completely convincing transformation, and when my students arrived for class I was slumped in a chair, a bottle of whiskey beween my legs, the torn lining of my miserable tuxedo hanging on the floor. No one said a word until I introduced myself. "Is Whitman still alive?" I heard one student ask another. I had memorized one of the poet's great Civil War poems and I stood up and recited it.

Then I walked to the door of the classroom and kicked it open. I stood in the threshold and bellowed, "Literature doesn't live in places like this! It lives on the lips of the dying soldiers! It lives in the passion of young men and women —" I can't recall the rest, but you get the idea. As I turned, a big football player rose to his feet and began to cheer. I paused, a little delirious, I suppose, wondering if he had seen the movie *Dead Poets Society,* where the students climb on top of their desks to applaud their departing professor. The rest of the students began clapping as I bowed graciously. Hiding behind my long gray beard I glanced up and down the corridor to see if my colleagues were hearing this. Three of them were standing outside the faculty lounge, looking in my direction. Take a good look at a real teacher, I thought. You can rot in this one-horse town, but I'm going places!

The only problem was this: that spring, fourteen of the twenty-three colleges where I'd applied rejected me. I had filled myself so full of hot air that I didn't see what this meant. Or maybe I did see, because each time a rejection letter arrived in the mail I was obsessed with getting rid of it. I would read the letter once, bury it at the bottom of the kitchen trash, and then take the trash bag with me and drop it into the dumpster behind the Creative Arts House on campus, where I was holding classes that semester.

One morning, a few days before graduation, I saw a guy in a white shirt and tie sitting in an unmarked car parked next to the dumpster. I waved to him as I dropped my trash bag in. An hour later came a visit from the head of security. "We've been trying to catch the person all semester," he said. "It was the diapers that made us sure it wasn't student trash."

I apologized and told him I'd pay whatever fine was required. "I've been fired," I told him. "I'm only here for three more days and I'm just trying to get out of town without punching anybody."

I was as surprised to say such a thing as he was to hear it said by a professor. He stepped away from me. "No, no," I told him, "I'm only kidding." But I don't think I was. For the first time I acknowledged to myself that I was behaving badly. The part of me that had always longed to be on the inside of the good life and was willing to make any concession to get there recognized that my future as an *employed* college professor depended in part upon the impression I left at Colgate. I knew that I should leave gracefully, shaking hands and giving best wishes to the people who had fired me.

But the newer part of me, the angry outsider who was just discovering the heady joy of giving the finger to authority, was the role I'd begun rehearsing in earnest. One night when a few students dropped by the house to say goodbye I told them about the dumpster incident. It was pretty late and we were standing out on the deck, where we could hear the distant roar of frat parties. I was holding center stage, telling my little story and hamming it up for the students when the lie just came on suddenly: "Yeah," I said, "you know what Hawthorne said about being an outsider. He said when you're an outsider, every hour you spend trying to get inside is an hour you should have spent learning to survive on the outside."

I'd made up the quote, and then I pushed it a little bit farther and said something profound about how maybe the way we deal with our trash defines us as insiders or outsiders. "I know this professor on University Avenue who's got this little cart that the trash cans sit in," I said disdainfully. "Can you believe that?"

"Hell," one of the students replied, "where I live, we go out to the suburbs and the rich people pay us to take away trash that they aren't allowed to put out on the curb. *Here's thirty bucks, kid. Get rid of this stuff, will you?* Sure! We take it away and dump it in the village green, then ride back into the city, laughing our asses off."

He started laughing, though the expression on his face said, *Man, you've been in your ivory tower so long, you don't have a friggin' clue about the outside!* And I laughed along with him, though I knew the joke was on me.

I began the morning of graduation day by locking myself in the sanctuary of the downstairs bathroom and reading the help wanted section in the *New York Times* for the first time in ten or twelve years. I discovered that while I had been away in the ivory tower the working world had been divided neatly — computer wizards on one end, nurses, sales clerks, and prison guards on the other. "Malls, prisons, or hospitals," I muttered. I didn't need the lousy help wanted pages anyway, I'd get my next great job from the professional journals. I crushed the pages into basketballs and fired bank shots off the shower stall into the wicker wastebasket. "What is a *systems analyst* anyway!" I yelled.

"What did you say, Daddy?" came a daughter's voice from another world.

I got down on my hands and knees, crawled quietly to the door, and yanked it open. "BOO!"

"Daddy!" Nell cried.

I kissed her and said, "Daddy's going to become a systems analyst, sweetheart. He's going to make a lot of money and everyone's going to be happy, happy, happy."

"Do we still have to move?" she asked.

Just as it was every year, the weather for the commencement exercises was perfect. At the end of the ceremony I walked the perimeter of the great green lawn, taking it all in again. Younger siblings and elderly relatives posing with the graduates while fathers folded their suit coats and began packing the station wagons and vans for the long trip home and back to work. I turned in my cap and gown at the faculty tent, then walked up the hill to Lawrence Hall to pack the last of my books. I was standing on my desk so I could reach the top shelf when I heard a young voice call to me from the doorway. "I just wanted to say goodbye," she said, and when I turned and looked at her, she added, "and good luck."

I shared with most of my male colleagues the unwritten rule never to be alone with a female student in a room with the door shut. "It gets hot in here," I always said as I kicked the door open. I climbed down from the desk.

"Why don't you leave the door open. It's really hot in here," I said.

She was wearing an amazing black sort of see-through blouse with what my grandmother used to call a plunging neckline.

"I probably smell like a brewery," she said. "Somebody threw champagne all over me."

She held her commencement cap in one hand and twirled the tassel with the other. "Well," I said, "it's a big day. Live it up."

I recalled that she had been planning to become a doctor, and she seemed genuinely surprised and touched that I remembered this. With an ironic smile she said she had given up the idea. "I think flunking organic chemistry my sophomore year kind of changed my mind," she said.

"What *are* you thinking of doing?" I asked her.

She told me she was going to work in her father's business. I've had many students hand me their résumés over the years, but she was the first to hand me her business card. It showed her name in black script below the name of the Ford dealership in bright blue letters.

"Great," I said.

She shrugged and said, "Not that great."

"Well, I mean the experience," I said.

She said, "Any kind of job is better than living at home, my mom and I would get along for the first few days and then it would be like high school."

I smiled at her.

"But if you ever need to buy a car . . ."

"Okay, that's nice," I told her.

She shrugged her shoulders again and glanced quickly around the office. Our eyes met. "I hope things work out for *you*," she said, looking at me with such a generosity of feeling that I briefly wondered if there was something left in this office, some trinket or small thing, that I could give to her.

"That's very kind," I said.

I expected her to say goodbye then and to walk out of my life forever, but she asked me if I was going to go back to Maine.

"We are," I replied.

"Will you see that soldier again?" she asked.

At first I didn't understand, but then she reminded me of a story I had told in class about a boy I'd grown up with in Bangor who went into the army. He and I had been in seventh grade together and were caught making faces at each other in science class. The teacher punished us by having us stand in front of the class and make faces for a whole period. Years later, when we were in high school and he was slotted into the building trades and I was in college prep, we lived in completely different worlds and we never talked, but whenever we would pass in the hallways we'd make faces at each other. He went to the war in Vietnam and I went to college.

"What happened to him?" she asked me.

I told her that I didn't know. "But before he left for boot camp we drank a six-pack of beer one night in the city park with the Paul Bunyon statue. He stood on my shoulders and climbed up on the statue and put the six tops from the beer cans on the ledge above one of Paul Bunyon's giant boots."

The room fell into silence for a little while and I sort of forgot that she was there until she asked me if he had died in the war. "I don't know," I said. Maybe I had told this story in class a dozen times across the years, but this was the first time I ever stopped to wonder what had become of him. I was embarrassed when I told her that I wasn't sure if he had survived the war or not.

"I don't know what happened to him," I told her. Then I smiled and thanked her again for dropping by. She paused in the doorway, shrugged her shoulders one last time, and said, "Anyway, the day you came to class dressed as Walt Whitman? I'll never forget that."

3

Packing and moving stamps your life hard with geometry. It's more than just the squares and rectangles of all the boxes. Carry a lamp shade in one hand, in the other a stack of Cat Stevens albums, and a football under one arm, and you suddenly see a triangle set in the landscape of your past. I caught myself carrying a wicker changing table up the ramp of the U-Haul truck and stepping right through the looking glass, back to the farmhouse in Iowa where I had bought it eight years earlier from a young couple who were selling everything they owned on a rainy morning after the farm had fallen out of their hands into bankruptcy. Then when I stood the changing table in one corner of the truck I was standing it up in the faculty apartment at Colby College, where I was teaching when Nell was born. I remembered a cold, cold winter, twenty-three below zero her first night home from the hospital. At night we'd wrap her in three receiving blankets with hoods and then pile our sweaters on top of her in the crib. When Colleen got up to feed her she would always have peed through all three layers of blankets. Colleen would change her as quickly as she could, wash her with a warm washcloth, wrap her up again, and feed her in our bed, laying her on her back between us while Colleen leaned over her so she could reach her nipples. As soon as Nell had filled her belly with warm milk she would poop through everything and Colleen would start over again, blowing on her fingers the whole time to warm them.

I was working my first college professor job in those days. We had come a long way since then. There had been better jobs and marvelous chances to live overseas. We had moved my firstborn daughter across seventeen states, the Atlantic Ocean, the Irish Sea, and the Mississippi River before she began first grade. Place a star over the point of each place we had slept together, calling it our home, and you would gaze upon the wildest constellation in the night sky. Name this constellation by the impulse that created it and you would name it *Desire.*

I loaded my arms like a man carrying firewood and lifted our possessions into the U-Haul truck. *The desire for what?* You ask yourself this question from time to time when your life is barreling along and there's not really time to answer it. The desire for more money, more security, more status, more respect, or more of a promise for more?

It was most likely all of the above. I was a member in good standing of the class of managerial mercenaries in my generation who moved anywhere for money, who called places *home* where we had no attachment to the land or the people, but where the opportunity for advancement was high.

It took most of the day to pack the truck. Nell, age six, had asked me to look for our manger set, since she'd been worried about the donkey all winter. What she really wanted was to be with me when I packed, but I insisted on doing it alone. Then as soon as I began the job I wished that I had made a family event out of it. To hell with all the great overbearing questions about myself, and to hell with all that was sad about this move, the kids could have carried the little things and we could have taken inventory together.

Most of the heavy objects in our life were gone now. I had come up with the idea of having a yard sale so we could travel lightly to wherever I was hired next. We had pared down our houseful of furniture to what was piled in front of me. We were back to where we had stood when we were first married, those days when we had little and it was hard for me to resist the rhapsodies of heavy appliances.

The day before, on the telephone, I had told the account manager for the retirement fund that we no longer owned anything I couldn't pick up and carry myself. I remember saying this proudly, and at the same time waiting expectantly for his reaction.

"Like the refugees," he said laconically.

I figured he was implying that the heavy objects we own — refrigerator, stove, the lumbering couch that requires two men and a boy to carry away — along with a retirement account, are the moorings that anchor us in the tricky currents of the grownup world, and without them a certain legitimacy is removed and we are more vulnerable to impulse, quicker to raise our voice at someone. Or to question ourselves. The whole world knows that you are only a boy until you own things that outweigh you.

Finally the truck was packed and the only thing left to do was to put the finishing touches on a birdhouse I was building. It was one of those bird hotels, actually, the kind that are intended to attract families of purple martins on their northward route each spring. I had built the thing with great care, a twelve-chambered hotel with a cedar-shingled roof and a wraparound porch supported by white columns. I had started out building it for my two oldest daughters, but in the end it became my intention to finish it and leave it behind for the geology professor who had bought our house.

Clouds were gathering as I dug the hole in the backyard where I would sink four feet of a sixteen-foot cedar post with the hotel fastened to the top on a wooden platform.

"It's too late," my neighbor called to me with what I felt was some pleasure. "You'll only get sparrows this time of year."

He went inside when it began to rain, and was probably watching me pick up the pieces after a gust of wind tore through the trees and blew the thing down. It took me a long time in the rain before I got it right. I stood on the deck admiring it and thinking it would stand as a monument to our brief residence on Maple Avenue. Then I went inside and stripped off my wet clothes in the bathroom off the kitchen. In the mirror I caught a glimpse of myself naked. It stopped me. When was the last time I had looked carefully at myself? Perhaps when I got dressed four years before to be interviewed for this job? I stood back and faced the firing squad. White skin. Muscles buried beneath pads of flesh. I had lived an indoor life for a long time, and it showed. I felt a quick rush of fear and I stood there long enough to wonder if my long effort to leave behind all the Snyder men who had labored with their hands to make their living had weakened me to the point that I might not be able to meet some price. I made a screwy face in the mirror, slumped my shoulders, stuck out my little potbelly and said, "Hello there, I'm Professor Milktoast."

* * *

It turned out that the manger had spent the winter in an old duffel bag where Colleen was saving baby clothes. I drove east with the donkey on the dashboard, my son in his Batman cape next to me, and next to him one daughter in charge of music. She got a pained look on her face every time I lifted the bottle of Kaopectate from between my knees and took another long slug. My stomach had been turning over wildly ever since the birdhouse fiasco. But by the time we crossed into Massachusetts I was singing with the kids and naming a prize for the first person to spot the WELCOME TO MAINE sign. "We'll call it the Neil R. Grabois Distinguished Lectureship in Nomadic Living Prize. And here's the first month's salary," I said, placing three quarters on the dashboard.

"Who's Neil—" asked Nell.

"The long-forgotten president of Colgate University," I said.

"I miss Colgate," Jack said.

I turned and saw the sadness in his eyes. It was a sadness that I was responsible for. I knew that, though he didn't. "Well," I said, "you don't want to miss it too much, Batboy, or you'll miss the sign!"

And it seemed like a personal welcome when we found that beneath the enormous WELCOME TO MAINE had been added, HOME OF THE NCAA ICE HOCKEY CHAMPIONS. I pulled the truck off the road and waited for Colleen to come up behind me in the station wagon. She had the camera. She kissed me and told us all where to stand for the photograph. I asked her to try and make sure she got wildflowers and the sardine plant in the background. Not the all-you-can-eats or factory outlets.

We were having fun when a pickup truck came speeding toward us with its horn blaring. I raised my hand in a big, open-hearted wave and the driver turned his head to look at me then gave me the finger as he flew by. "What the hell?" I muttered. I gathered up the kids, piled them into the station wagon, and told Colleen to drive carefully. I never got a good look at him. I tried to dismiss him as just another one of the knuckleheads that Maine is famous for, guys who can end up one of only two ways — they either go to the penitentiary or they become state troopers. I could picture this clown with a knife on his belt and his jeans slung so low on his narrow hips that when he bent over he showed the crack of his behind to the whole world. I dismissed him with the same scorn that I'd always dismissed guys like him, but when I got back into the truck I sat there behind the wheel for a long time just looking down the highway. I began to feel the same rush of fear I had experienced standing in front of the mirror.

I got back on the interstate and drove along thinking what it would be like to catch up with him and give *him* the finger, maybe force him off the road and have it out with him. I thought about this in minute detail for the next half hour or so, imagining what I would say to him, playing the scene forward and then reversing and starting over again, revising the scene until I *was* saying everything to him that I wanted, *needed* to say. Maybe I'd tell him that I'd been making myself better than guys like him from as far back as I could remember. I'd made myself into a star athlete so I could get ahead of him. That was part of the escape velocity that had carried me forward. Hell, didn't he know who I *was?* I spent my twenties, before I met Colleen, picking up velocity by consciously transforming myself into a far more extraordinary man than the punks and working stiffs below me. I wanted my life to be important. And how could it be unless I was doing important work? So I made the headlines and the evening news for everyone to see; I was twenty-seven when I quit my job as a newspaper editor and set out on a mission to clear the name of a dead soldier from the Korean War whom the army had convicted and sent to prison as a traitor during the McCarthy era. All his life the man had claimed he was innocent and then he died before he could prove it. I met him just before his final heart attack and I spent the next seven years battling the United States Army, the FBI, and the CIA and traveling back and forth across the country until I found the men who had testified against him at his court-martial in 1955. I persuaded the army's chief prosecution witnesses to come forward and confess that they had been pressured by their commanding officers to frame this soldier from Maine. Then I pressured the FBI to release their secret intelligence reports on the man, which had falsely portrayed him as a communist. I found the commanding officers who were to blame and finally I forced the Secretary of the Army to hold a public hearing at the Pentagon. I did all this because the dead soldier had left behind a son who never fully believed that his father was innocent. I brought the son to Washington for the hearing so he could see the truth about his father.

Why? I asked myself as I drove along. I had always believed my motives were honorable, right down to when Hollywood bought the rights to the book I'd written about this story and I split the money evenly with the soldier's widow.

But now I wondered if I had done it in order to prove something about myself. To prove perhaps that I deserved a celebrated life and the kind of comfortable university position such a public accomplishment would win me. I cared, of course I cared about the soldier and his family. I cared deeply. But it came to me as I drove up the interstate that I had always been someone who picked his battles carefully, always calculating what they would be worth to me in the long run.

All of that was running through my head, and when I snapped out of it I couldn't remember stopping to pay the toll.

We had found a handsome, sprawling Maine farmhouse in the town of Yarmouth and rented it sight unseen for the summer. It was exactly what I had been hoping for all along even though it cost twice what a house in the neighborhood of Colleen's parents would have cost. As I beheld the place for the first time it looked like the kind of house where a successful man would live. A house near the ocean, where he would place his family in comfort and style for the summer months, just long enough for him to land a new job.

When we pulled into the driveway, two of Colleen's brothers and her mother and father and two sisters were there to greet us. An old friend of mine from down the road showed up with pizza and beer just in time to help me lug the mattresses up to the third floor. We were walking through the empty rooms when he asked me why I'd moved back to Maine.

"It's home," I told him.

"Yeah," he said, "but I mean why'd you leave Colgate?"

"Too far from the Atlantic Ocean," I said, my voice echoing off the bare walls and floor. "When we went out there we thought we'd stay for two years. We stayed for four. Too long." This reason for having returned to Maine, invented that first hour back, would become my stock answer to all who inquired why Colleen and I had come back home from the place we had moved to so hopefully four years before. I gave the reason often enough and so casually that I had myself half convinced I hadn't been fired.

I see now that I should have been feeling real fear over our situation. Not only because, one by one, during those first weeks

43

back in Maine, I was turned down for seven more of the professor-ships I had applied for, but because even these rejections and the fact that I had only two colleges left to hear from didn't spark in me any emotion more urgent than a desire to conceal the letters from Colleen. There was an old Ben Hogan golf bag in the barn, and when each letter arrived I read it, folded it into a small square, and dropped it to the bottom of the golf bag.

In spite of all my introspection, I didn't see anything the way it actually was, though I did have the profound suspicion that the world might have changed. I thought again and again about the story my student from the Bronx had told me that night on my porch, the story of how he and his buddies used to dump people's trash in the village greens of the nice suburbs. More than any-thing else, that student stayed in my thoughts. It was the way he had told the story to me, that look of satisfaction on his face, as if he were disabusing me of some illusion I held.

Still, it was summer in Maine and it felt good to be back. I climbed the stairs and in the front bedroom found Colleen and all four kids asleep in the same bed. They were all so beautiful and peaceful that it took my breath away. The three girls were sucking their thumbs and I took them out of their mouths and then lifted Jack off the corner of the bed, where he had soaked the sheets. "Jackie boy," I whispered as I carried him to the bathroom. I stood him up in front of the toilet and he wobbled like a little drunk. I remembered how shocking his anatomy was to me when he came out of Colleen. With two daughters, I hadn't expected a son. He turned out to be a ten-pounder with wide shoulders, a head of thick black hair, and red cheeks, and when he first ap-peared to me he looked like he'd just stopped by on his way from a convention of miniature Irish politicians. But it was a diffi-cult delivery. Forceps didn't work, and a horrendous vacuum cleaner–type machine failed to suck him out. All at once the doctor summoned help. Suddenly there were all these people in the delivery room attending to Colleen and urging her on. I stood off to one side, useless and glad for their help. Colleen in her pain and determination was as beautiful and aloof as the moon.

Back in the bedroom I put Cara in her crib so there was room in bed for me. I noticed then that Colleen had taken the time to hang the needlepoint murals she had made for each of the kids near the end of each pregnancy. The moon and stars against a cobalt blue sky. The lobster boat with a flock of white gulls overhead. I couldn't remember ever seeing her working on these murals; it was as if they had just appeared. Where had she found the time? I wondered.

I knew that she was trying now to make this strange room look like home to her children. I looked down at her before I got into bed. There, I thought. All you have to do is follow her example. She isn't drifting back to the past or racing ahead into the future, she is just *here, now,* for her children. I didn't want to step forward and join the ranks of those pathetic men who hit a middle-age roadblock and immediately start looking around for somebody to blame or for some great truth hidden in the past — a truth that more closely resembles an excuse when you hold it to the light. I'd lost my job. All I wanted to do was dump our stuff in this rented house, shake the dust off my shoes, find a way back to the passing lane, and punch the accelerator down. I'd always wanted a clean break from the past. Hell, doesn't success depend on this?

I had just fallen asleep when Cara began crying. I went to her crib so she wouldn't wake everyone. Over the years with babies you develop a way of sifting their cries, like when people used to have the party line telephone system and you knew which ring was yours and which rings you could ignore. This was a cry for reassurance, a cry that always struck me as most urgent, and at the same time, the easiest to mollify. Coming downstairs with Cara in my arms, my game plan was to put some milk in her bottle, give it to her and rock her for a few minutes, and then pop her back in her crib. I'd done this a hundred times across the years, without a thought in my head, and sometimes in my sleep. But when I opened the door of the refrigerator and looked down at Cara, I was suddenly overcome by the feeling of my own weight settling and of everything around me dropping into slow motion. I guess it was the velocity draining out of me for the first time since I'd begun racing toward a successful life twenty-five years earlier. And for once, I didn't hurry my daughter back to bed. Instead I showed her the moon, its thick light like syrup pouring through the windows of the old house and spilling across the lawns. I felt grains of sand on the pine floor beneath my bare feet, sand from someone else's trips to the beach.

When we went outside, I thought, *Let me slow down and live this moment with you the way your mother does. Here, let me show you where we are, not where we are going.* We moved through the deep relief of shadows. Shadows tangled and swaying in the breeze. I thought about the night I had carried her across campus and shown her the big banners with my name on them. I hadn't asked myself any questions then, I was on automatic pilot, and so that night already seemed to belong to another life that happened a long time ago and wasn't mine.

I kept telling myself just to mark this passage so I would remember the far-off train whistle ten miles south at the freight yard, and the crickets at our feet that stopped their screech when we passed. At the end of the driveway a skunk hobbled off into the tall grass like an old shoplifter disappearing behind a coat rack. Cara was silent, curved and pressed against me. Looking down at her I caught her smile. Why shouldn't I still be astonished by her? Here was her faint voice speaking her first little sentences, and yet there was her foot still small enough to wash in a teacup.

Twenty-seven steps to the main road. We didn't cross it. Instead we pretended there was another country on the other side, a country that didn't invite trespassers. But from where we stopped we could see the running lights on boats moored in the river. The scent of saltwater mudflats rose up the hill. There was the gurgle of a pump, sucking bilgewater and spilling it back. I lifted her so she could see the band of moonlight on the water, and when this light caught her diaper and her white ditchdigger T-shirt, she was luminous, like an infant dressed for baptism.

The backyard sloped up steeply. I felt my breath shorten. Eighty nine-steps to the top, where a badminton net caught us like a spiderweb. We snuck like Indians into the woods. I felt a mushroom and then moss, pine needles, old leaves, rotting bark under my feet. I brushed her cheek against the cool leaves of a hanging branch. She reached out and grabbed a fistful to carry the rest of the way.

The latch on the barn door was wet with dew. I took her inside and walked amid old snow tires, half a roll of asbestos insulation, five rusted metal tackle boxes, the leather case of an old camera left behind like the skin of a snake. There was a baseball bat for me to swing, a Hula-Hoop, rugs rolled up and covered with dirt. Three cane chairs with their seats missing. Moths in the two windows. A June bug batting against the glass. A carpenter's workbench.

Normally I'd be hurrying to get to bed to get some sleep for the workday ahead and I wouldn't have noticed the weathervane on the roof, its arrow aiming toward the southwest. *Here,* I said to my daughter, *let me tell you where you are.* I began by pointing her to the south and I named the cousins sleeping there and a grandmother who had been a nurse for thirty years and a great-grandmother who crossed the sea from Ireland seventy-two years ago. She was at the farthest reach of my daughter's life. A quarter turn back to the south, another grandfather was at work on the dock where the oil tankers tie up. Cara looked like him, her mother's father. He had her mother for his daughter, and then his daughter re-created him in her own daughter. West and north another tribe of cousins, aunts, and uncles. Friends everywhere I turned, and as I named them all I kept spinning around until her smile became a grin. Surrounded by relatives, I felt as if I had boomeranged through time so that I was now standing in the midst of those men I had run from. I thought of my aunt Francis, who contracted polio at the state fair when she was seven, and her father, my uncle Walter, a garage mechanic, who carried her like a doll from her wheelchair to her bed and to the bathroom for sixty years. She lived her whole life beneath his roof and he still did push-ups when he was seventy-nine in order to keep his arms and shoulders strong so he could carry his daughter. In his endless aching sadness, there must have been some part of him that rejoiced in this closeness, and another part that was astonished each time he looked and saw that the infant he had once carried was now the old woman in his arms. He carried her from bed to her wheelchair ten minutes before he died. In the unfamiliar slowness of this night I felt connected to him; it was as if he were a link to my daughter's future. I wondered when she would be carried in her life. My hope was only that she would never be carried against her will, and that she would never be carried broken or wounded, but if it came to that, that she be carried gently. And I knew that she would be shaped by what she carried in her life just as Uncle Walter's arms and shoulders were shaped by carrying his daughter for more than sixty years. I wanted Cara to carry the memory of this night as well.

When I looked down at her again, she was sleeping. To the west that June night, beyond the shadows of our trees and barn, there were lights on in a few of the houses across the valley. Small pinpricks of light in the darkness. A modern man on the make knows little about his neighbors, and I had barely memorized their names in the different places where we had lived, but tonight I felt a peculiar sympathy with the people asleep around me. How small *we all are* in the darkness in the dead of night, I thought. And how ferocious our urge to light our way. Sometimes we don't even know the weight of what we're carrying ourselves in our need to claim and reclaim our own lives. I looked at my daughter and hoped that in her life as a woman she would find moments like this one, moments of being, when what was right next to her was enough to keep her from asking for more. I hoped that she would not be carried off by the desires that had carried me from place to place, never satisfied, always waiting for life to match my expectations.

4

Pension check after taxes $13,600.

Plus savings $3,401 = $17,001.

MINUS: *Summer rent $3,000 in advance. Truck rental $546.30. Telephone $84.14. Food $218.17. Firewood $125. Car registration $61.50. Miscellaneous $114.98.*

BALANCE *June 6: $12,850.91*

My head cleared and I left all the deep, depressing thoughts behind and hit my stride again when, in the third week of June, four new positions were advertised in the professional journals. This brought my chances to six. I suspected these four new ones were last-minute openings caused by illness, death, or newly allocated sums of money, and because the field of applicants would be narrow at this stage of the game and the interviewing committees would be eager to wrap things up so they could disperse for the summer, it was not beyond the realm of possibility that I could nail down one of these jobs in two weeks' time. A done deal!

The only thing I allowed to dampen my enthusiasm was the faint acknowledgment that the reason I'd been rejected by twenty-one colleges in the fifteen months since Colgate fired me was because I was not a woman or a minority applicant. There was nothing exotic about my dossier and I knew perfectly well that white male professors in English departments were as plentiful as shopping mall Santa Clauses, and their credibility was threatened incrementally each time a new white male was welcomed aboard and issued a red suit. I began to wonder if this had become a deciding issue since I was last in the job market, in 1988, when I'd had the luxury of turning down offers from five universities to sign on at Colgate.

Still, I had high hopes. The days were long and we spent them together on the beaches, where Cara took her first steps and Nell and Erin learned to ride the waves and I was teaching Jack to catch a baseball. Usually members of Colleen's family joined us for these excursions and at the end of the day we would pick somebody's house to meet at for a cookout. On rainy days we would get a fire burning in the fireplace and play Parcheesi and Monopoly. And whenever I spotted a glum expression I would head out to the mall to buy presents for everyone. I loved the moment when I would stand at the front door, my arms loaded with gifts, and everyone would rush toward me yelling with excitement. My purchases were modest at first, little plastic toys that often didn't make it through the first hour home. But then they grew more elaborate — jewelry, soccer balls, dolls, a board hockey game, sundresses. Only later did I discover that Colleen was hiding the things I bought for her in a downstairs closet and then returning them for cash. "Save the receipts," she always said to me in the midst of each celebration; it never dawned on me that she was worrying about money. She didn't tell me at first because she didn't want to hurt my feelings; she must have known from the start that bringing home prizes for her and the children bolstered the image I had of myself as a successful father and husband. This was the same image I was trying to preserve by hiding my job rejection letters from her.

Image was certainly part of the reason I kept buying things, but even more than that, I think the shopping was a relief simply because it gave me someplace to go.

In the case of Nell, who was six years old, it was something more complicated. In a large family you have times when you are closer to one child than the others. I suppose this can be explained by any number of reasons, but in the case of Nell, it was her preternatural affection for animals of any size and stripe. So focused and unwavering was this affection that she often had vivid dreams about a dog or cat or hamster that had come of its own volition to take up residence in her bedroom. This aspect of her personality made it easy to relate to her under any circumstance; I could fill any silence between us simply by starting a conversation about animals. During one trip to the mall I found a little mechanical white dog with battery-powered legs and a bark that enchanted her for hours and hours. She named the dog Pup, and when she began to shape her daily schedule around his grooming and feeding and to sleep with him on her pillow I began to worry constantly about the day when he would break and her small determined heart would break along with him. I wanted to be able to prolong the time in my life when I would be singularly capable of making this daughter smile. And since I wasn't at work all day and I had nothing else to concentrate my energies on, I would have gone to any length and spent any amount of money or time to keep her from being sad.

During a stretch of three rainy days in a row when the kids all grew homesick for Hamilton, New York, I brought home new bicycles for everyone. This was Jack's first bike, and I hoped it would distract him from his loneliness for the best friend he had left behind. Almost every day he would report to me or his mother that he had heard Brian Murphy's voice out behind the barn or under his bed. "You learn how to ride this bike, and someday you and Brian can ride together," I promised him. But he took a bad spill during one of our first practise sessions and he screamed at me through a hurricane of tears and screeches, "Saw that stupid bike in half!"

One afternoon I was searching for a gravel road that would take us to a special beach that I remembered from years before. When, at last, it seemed that we were there and I began to turn onto a narrow lane, I spotted, just ahead a little ways, a gatehouse with a uniformed cop inside with his hand raised. I quickly turned us back out onto the main road. "We'll go to another beach," I announced to the kids.

"When are we gonna *get there!*" Jack yelled from the third seat of the station wagon, where we had to keep him in order to give his three sisters some relief from his pestering.

Colleen turned to me with the timeless expression that said, *Don't look at me, he's your son too.*

"What about McDonald's for a treat?" I asked Colleen.

It was how she turned away and stared out the window. "What? No treat for the kids?" I said.

"There are six of us," she said. "It's expensive. Plus—"

"There have been six of us for quite a while now," I told her.

"For the money I could make us a much better meal."

"Why don't you come in with us," I said. "We can all eat inside."

She told me she wasn't hungry. I looked at her, loving the way a few strands of her hair brushed across one cheek, and across the other, a single thin braid. We'd been together twelve years but her beauty still surprised me. When she leaned forward and took the wallet from the glove compartment I saw her ribs through the opening between the buttons of her blouse. She had been denying that she was losing weight, but it was obvious.

"What about a milk shake," I pleaded.

"I'm not hungry," she said.

"Well you still need to eat. You don't eat anything anymore."

She sighed and handed me the wallet. "You didn't write in the checkbook what you spent for the bicycles," she said.

Her accusation reached me just as I was thinking I would hold her face in my hands and look right into her eyes and undress her slowly as soon as we were alone, in order to show her that everything was all right.

"Are we *there yet!*"

"Hey, *you!*" I yelled to Jack. "Put a cork in it, will you!" I looked back at Colleen until she turned away.

I let the kids out of the back, and while they charged inside I went to Colleen's window and asked her again to come inside with us.

"I'm not hungry," she said.

"I know," I said. "The bikes cost three hundred and something."

"That's a lot of money," she said. "The girls were happy with their old bikes."

I looked at her. "Okay," I said. And then I walked away, wanting to convince her of something. At that moment I thought that maybe I should spend every penny we had left, taking us right up to the edge before landing a new job just in time and refilling our savings account while Colleen's faith in me was renewed. That's what it was — I wanted to convince her to keep her faith in me.

The next few minutes, waiting in line at McDonald's, marked the beginning of a new period of confusion. Inside the golden arches, we were pressed together beneath an enormous banner that proclaimed, "DRIVE-THROUGH BREAKFAST!"

"Now there's a dream come true," I said louder than I'd intended.

"What?" the guy beside me asked harshly.

"Nothing," I said with a smile. I looked away, and when I looked back he was eyeing me warily. I wondered what he saw. I wondered if he thought I was someone he needed to keep an eye on. What came over me was this peculiar sense of leaning back too far. I felt off balance, like I was standing on a table and the table was being tilted slightly, or like I was wearing shoes with the heels worn down in back. I thought about how I would go through the mail as soon as we got home, maybe finding another letter that said, "Thank you anyway for your application . . . We will keep your file active in the event . . ." I would file it away in the golf bag with the others I had already received. We were packed inside the glass walls. The kids had been swept away to a cash register at the opposite end of the counter. I was reading a button on the cashier's brown blouse — "WE WANT TO BE YOUR HOME AWAY FROM HOME" — when suddenly I was leaning back again. I reached for something to steady myself. The man next to me moved away. I looked around at the brightly colored signs, smiling cheeseburgers, and dancing soft drinks. I looked at the other fathers and wondered if any of them felt like they were falling backwards, caught in an undertow.

"It wasn't my idea to stop there," Colleen said to me a few days later when I tried to explain how I had felt inside McDonald's. I was sitting at the workbench in the barn with a new badminton set on my lap. Colleen stood in the doorway. There was a blue sky behind her.

"I know that," I said. "I know it was my idea." I didn't want to make too much of it, but I wanted to explain to her the feeling of falling backwards. I had figured it out and I wanted her to know. I said to her, "It's like I've spent my whole life climbing this ladder, trying to get up high enough so I could see beyond my father's life. Not just *his* life, but the life that was intended for me too. He used to take us to McDonalds after it opened in Bangor. He always made a big deal out of it, like, *This is as good as it gets, so I hope you appreciate it.* I always ordered milk because I hated the powdered milk we had to drink at home. He always mixed it very thin so that it was half the price of real milk. It wasn't white in the glass, it was a pale bluish gray. The same color of our windows in the winter when he tacked plastic to them to keep out the cold."

I told Colleen that maybe what I felt was the ladder wobbling beneath me. "Maybe that happens once you stop climbing even for a minute."

"You won't fall," she said sweetly. "You'll keep climbing. You always have."

I was so grateful for her understanding that even when I caught her searching the badminton box to see how much I had paid for it at Toys R Us, I reached out and touched her. She stepped the rest of the way inside the barn and pulled the door closed behind her.

Even with her in my arms I went on feeling the momentum of my life falling away from me. And I think that I kept returning to the mall to try and catch up with the bewildering movement *forward* that America had become and that I was no longer a part of. I loved watching the young people in their wild clothes, though they made me homesick for a college campus. I watched an employee about my age at Hickory Farms cutting beefstick samples. I wondered how long he had done this job, and if he dressed for work each day with a sense of dread. Could I do his job? I wondered. If I did his job wouldn't I be falling back a little closer to my father's world each day?

One day I followed a perfume trail to Victoria's Secret, a store I had never in my life entered. It didn't take long to figure out that all the merchandise in the store was really for men. "Would you like our catalog?" the sales clerk said archly as she handed me one. She was heartbreakingly beautiful. "Some people call it the poor man's *Playboy*," she told me with a knowing smile. I took it. On the cover a woman was looking down at her nipples in a see-through bra. I looked back at the clerk. She sort of nodded at me as if to say, *Yes, this can be yours, even though you are not bringing home a paycheck and you spend your days walking around the mall.*

I stood over a table where pastel-colored panties were spread out like candy. I backed away and knocked up against neatly stacked towers of cassette tapes — music to make love by. I thought about a nightgown for Colleen, but they were all too flimsy for the chill of Maine evenings.

I was pawing through a selection of tights when two women with piano bench legs emerged from a dressing room. "Did it show a little crotch, though?" one of them asked hopefully. "I want to show a little crotch."

"Can I help you with anything?" another clerk asked me. She was gorgeous too. She caught me looking at the black lace from her bra, which lay against the white skin below her throat. She possessed the confidence that only expert training can account for, and I believed she had heat-seeking missiles designed to lock onto the target with the least amount of self-respect. "Are you looking for something for your wife?" she asked.

"Yes," I replied weakly.

"These are nice," she told me when she spun around a carousel of stockings. She looked at me with such a sympathetic expression that I half expected her to pull up her miniskirt and try on a pair for me. *You can have this,* her eyes said. *You're down on your luck right now, I can tell, but you can still have this.*

I bought a pair and then stopped at Sears and stared at tires for a while to clear my head.

The next morning I put the stockings on the pillow next to Colleen's head. I wanted to wake her and tell her not to worry about anything. Her shoulders were freckled from the sun, and in the early light I could see the dark red in her hair. I lay there looking at her, my desire for her increasing like slowly mounting snow. I didn't want to make love to her so much as ask her if she was happy. But it was too early for that. Instead I walked down the hill to the boatyard and sat on the dock. The harbor was as still as a pond. The boats were turned at their moorings, facing the same direction like cows in a field.

I stopped at the bakery and bought Colleen a jelly donut. When I got back home the house was still quiet but she was awake, lying peacefully in a band of sunlight that reached across the bed.

"Thank you," she said. "I haven't worn stockings since my first communion."

I waited for a few seconds, then leaned down and kissed her.

"Maybe you should get some exercise," she said.

"Really?"

"When I first met you, you played sports all the time, and now you really don't do anything."

"Well, I used to work," I said defensively.

That day I ended up at a baseball field running around like a clown in centerfield, trying to chase down fly balls in my penny loafers. I came upon the field when I was taking a bike ride for exercise, and I was resting in the dugout when two ballplayers arrived with a bucket of baseballs and a bat to take their practice. They had a big game coming up. "If you let me use your glove," I said, "I'll shag balls for you." This didn't seem preposterous to them at all. The lanky kid just tossed his glove to me and I trotted to the outfield. I got under the first ball perfectly, but somehow it cut sharply to the left just as I was about to catch it and it hit me like a rock squarely on my right shoulder. I tried to conceal my surprise and the pain, but the kid who was pitching called out to me to see if I was all right. It got worse. I tripped over my feet and fell running back to the fence. I missed all but two. Two catches out of about sixty balls. I was out there for an hour and it wasn't coming back to me when we quit. It didn't bother me that my lungs were burning and my legs were sore, I expected the physical failure. But what I couldn't believe was that I had lost my ability to judge a baseball's flight across the sky. This had come naturally to me from the first time I tried it. I had been able to stand in center field 350 feet from where the batter stood, and when he took his practice swings I would anticipate where the ball would go if he connected, and this way I'd get a jump on the ball. I'd been scouted by three major league teams during my college career. Playing against the University of Maine one afternoon I ran ten or fifteen strides with my back to the ball, reached up and took it out of the sky as it was still rising, hit the fence at top speed, but held on to the ball. The scout for the Pittsburgh Pirates watching the game told my coach he only knew of three center fielders who could have made that catch and all three of them were in the big leagues.

That was gone. Every bit of it. Still, when we were finished and the ballplayers walked off the field to the parking lot I shut my eyes and listened to the clinking of their spikes on the cement, and the sound brought back to me a part of life I had lived, and something I had known and been a part of. I looked around at the scuffed planks on the floor of the dugout, the bench with its layers of peeling green paint. The grass and the dirt. Sitting there made me suddenly lonely for Colleen. Not only for her company but for some knowledge of her past. I knew so little about her, really. I'd never asked her what games she had played as a young girl, or what she was afraid of, or if she missed those days when we first met. I thought about how she laughed, and then I couldn't remember the last time I'd heard her laugh. And hadn't she sung to herself when I first met her? When I got home I asked her out on a date. I promised her a movie and maybe a piece of cheesecake at a local restaurant, but as I was going through the garage to go get the baby-sitter I picked up the baseball bat and the Texaco bucket filled with old tennis balls and threw them into the back of the station wagon with our picnic blanket.

At the Little League field Colleen hit me fly balls for a while, but they really weren't high enough or long enough to change anything. Finally I asked her if she would mind pitching to me. We did this until it was dark, then we ended up in each other's arms in center field, lying in the damp grass, surrounded by yellow tennis balls.

"It's too late for the movies now," she said.

"Tomorrow night, then," I said.

We talked about a summer night when the fireflies were so thick in a meadow near our house that we woke Erin and Nell and carried them from their beds to see. We'd done a lot of things like that, we both agreed, holding the kids up to things we knew they were too young to remember, but holding them anyway.

"I'm going to start looking for a job tomorrow," she said. "A waitress job, I think."

This came as a complete surprise and sent me tilting backwards. I could only think of being left in charge of the kids myself, being stuck in the house with nothing to do, making lunch in an egg-stained bathrobe. I asked her not to. "Everything is changing," I said. "I can feel it. The kids need one thing not to change. Please." I thought about all the rejection letters I had disposed of in the dumpster at Colgate and the others that were hidden in the golf bag. I thought of the remaining schools I hadn't heard from and I asked her to promise me that she wouldn't talk again about getting a job. "Please," I said again. "If you start looking for a job I'm going to think it's because you don't think I'll get one. Promise me you won't think that." I looked right into her eyes when I said this.

"Maybe I should have worked all these years instead of having babies," she said.

She suddenly looked very sad. I let her go on. She talked for a while about how fulfilled she felt at home with the children but how she worried sometimes that they might think less of her one day for not having a career the way many other mothers had. "They might think I've been lazy," she said.

"Not a chance," I said.

I was looking for some pity, so I told her about my experience at the ball field that afternoon. "I was trying as hard as I could," I explained, "but I couldn't catch a baseball. I mean, Jesus, how can that be?"

"Well," she said sweetly, "you can still hit."

She lay back in my arms and sighed. "I loved everything about being pregnant," she said. "What I miss most are my big boobs."

"Big boobs are overrated," I said. "And after eight years of breast-feeding, aren't you sort of glad it's over?"

"No. I'll miss it for the rest of my life," she told me.

I looked down at her and told her that we didn't know what would happen. "We might have another baby someday," I said.

She let this pass, and then she said, "I know some things. Things that you don't know."

"Like what?" I asked.

She shook her head. "Never mind," she said.

5

I began to feel uncomfortable sitting at the beach because it was the sort of thing we used to do on vacation and I wasn't on vacation, and because men who are supporting their families don't spend day after day at the beach. Eventually we fell into our separate routines. Each morning I would sit at a desk drinking coffee and going over copies of the letters I had written to colleges while Colleen gathered the kids and their things for the daily pilgrimage. The picnic lunch would be packed (*"Should I make your peanut butter and jelly sandwiches?"* Colleen calls to me), and the search for Jack's swimming trunks would begin again in earnest, and pretty soon I would be standing at the station wagon waving goodbye, watching them until they are out of sight. Then I would fight off a chill of sadness while I got on my bicycle and rode to the Little League field on the outskirts of town where I kept my bucket of tennis balls and a Mickey Mantle thirty-five-inch bat underneath the dugout. For two or three hours I would stand at home plate and hit the balls, fungo-style, into the empty outfield. I'd swing for all I was worth while my mind went through the list of schools to which I had applied for teaching work and from which I was waiting to hear. And when I stopped to pick up the balls in the outfield I dreamed about moving my children back to one of those heavenly college towns where there were overarching shade trees that would turn yellow and red in autumn, and a movie theater where we'd go some Saturday to see Walt Disney's *Old Yeller,* and a drugstore with a soda fountain, and on one corner a florist where I would pick up roses for Colleen on my way home from class.

One morning when I arrived at the ball field, a man was hitting golf balls into the outfield. I swore at him under my breath, and went back home. Then when I returned a couple days later he was there again.

It came on slowly between the two of us, the way it often does between men. A wave of his hand and soon I was telling him about how I ought to be at the beach with my wife and my four kids. "I was fired from my job and I'm trying to figure out some things," I said. "It's hard to concentrate unless I'm alone."

"Hey," he said kindly, "I know what you mean."

He had been out of work for over two years, since his development company went bankrupt during the real estate bust in southern Maine. Excommunicated from the country club, he played his golf now in the outfield of this deserted Little League park. He wore a bright red Chicago Bulls cap and a short-sleeved madras shirt. I noticed his hands looked as soft and unwrinkled as a child's, but I figured him to be around sixty. He had set up an imaginary par three golf course and he believed he was getting his swing back. "I couldn't go back to work now even if I had a chance to," he told me. "I've lost so much weight, none of my suits fit me anymore."

I admired his good nature and began to look forward to seeing him each day, and after three or four days he brought along an extra golf club for me and I played around with him. I happened to mention one day that I was going to Boston for a reunion with my best friends and that I was a little nervous about facing them without any concrete job prospects. "I know the story," he said. "A man with no prospects can't spare a minute to relax."

He had put his finger on my feelings so precisely that I felt encouraged enough to go on and tell him about the odd sensation I'd been having, the feeling of leaning back on my feet as if I were going to topple over.

"I've been there too," he said. "You've got to remember it's not your fault; you didn't screw the dean's wife, did you? No. It's the whole friggin' country now. A man can't get a break anymore. Not a *white man,* at least. Remember this — whenever you feel like blaming yourself, take a look around, it's not you, it's the damned *system.* Communism went bust, and we're all so busy gloating about that, we can't see that we're next. The civilization is in decline, my friend. These are bad times and it's not your fault."

Music to my ears! It was a relief to lay the blame for my uneasiness at the feet of *the system* and to walk away from any personal responsibility for what was happening. But I was still worried about facing my friends, and three days before the reunion I told Colleen that I had decided not to go. "I don't really feature showing up there with my tail between my legs," I said to her one night after the kids had gone to bed and she was folding laundry on the couch.

She didn't understand. "They're your best friends in the world," she said.

I was watching her hands as she matched the children's socks and folded their dresses and shirts. She had a pile for each child, and she knew which pieces of clothing belonged to whom. This seemed amazing to me. I wondered where I had been when she had purchased these clothes and what I had been doing when she had taught our children how to dress themselves. It seemed to me then that somewhere across the last few years I had accepted the fact that I would never know our children in the way she knew them and that I would never be able to account for the passage of so much time.

I came out and told her about all the job rejections. "You never asked," I said, "but there have been twenty-one so far."

"That's okay," she said. "You'll find a job. I know that and so do your friends."

I looked at the piles of clothing. "Everything is still so small," I said, taking a few white T-shirts to fold.

"Not as small as it used to be," she said.

"Yeah, but they still have a long way to go," I said. I put my face against a little ruffled dress and breathed in the scent of baby powder. I held the dress out to her. "Take a smell," I said.

She smiled and asked me if I remembered Erin wearing the dress when we lived in Iowa.

"Sure," I said. But I didn't. I'd forgotten.

She said, "I guess I'll have to give these baby things away after Cara outgrows them."

I looked at her and thought for sure that she was waiting for me to deny this. "Are we out of the baby business?" I asked.

She looked into my eyes, smiled, and shrugged her shoulders. "I don't know," she said. "If we are, though, don't tell me. Okay?"

"Okay," I said.

"And when you go to Boston to see your friends, you don't have to pretend you're not scared."

"Scared of what?" I asked. "I mean I *am* scared."

She looked deeply troubled by this. Finally she said to me, "Just be yourself, that's all I meant."

I thought about this all the way to Boston, riding the Greyhound bus while my friends made their way to the reunion. Jim Robinson, a lawyer now in Florida, would fly into Boston. Johnny Woodcock, also an attorney, and John Bradford, an orthopedic surgeon, would drive down to Boston from Bangor, Maine, where they lived and worked. Jim Wright would fly in from San Francisco, where he was dean at a college. In the beginning, in eighth grade, Bradford was a chubby boy with a round face and red hair, one of those gregarious kids who smiled at every waitress as if he were falling in love with her or as if he thought he had to win her love before she would give him a menu. Robinson was a fighter with a quick wit and fast fists. Woodcock, the fourth child in a family of seven children, was a thinker, and from the moment he deciphered the words in the hit record "Louie, Louie," the four of us assumed he was in touch with a greater authority than we'd ever encountered. Big Jim Wright walked with long, purposeful strides that matched his personality.

I had earned my way into their world from the poor side of the city by scoring touchdowns and hitting home runs and being lucky, and once I beheld the splendor of their lives — the maids who cleaned their houses, their kitchen pantries stocked with food, their great open yards for football games, their convertibles and summer camps on the ocean, their lawyer and doctor fathers — I wanted to be a part of it. Bradford's house had an attached barn with a basketball court in the loft big enough to have a basket at both ends! To reach the back stairs that led to the barn you passed through the den, where there was a bell-shaped glass jar filled with hard candy, and if there was no one watching, I always stopped and filled my pockets. Amazingly the jar was refilled again and again, and this one small detail fueled my desire to prove myself worthy of a world where grown-ups had extra money and nice things.

That desire led me, when I turned seventeen, to the island of Martha's Vineyard, for my first job as a dishwasher in a summer hotel. By the time I was twenty I had been promoted high enough to secure jobs for my friends so we could spend what turned out to be our last summer together before wives and babies and jobs took us in different directions. We lived together that summer in the help's quarters on the fourth floor of the hotel, a few doors away from dozens of beautiful waitresses, barmaids, cocktail hostesses, and chambermaids, all college girls from across the country. It was a dream and it had convinced me and my friends that I had it within my power to make good things happen. It was the proof I had needed to be certain that my life was meant to be extraordinary.

That's who I am, I thought. *I'm someone who's always pulled through. That's who I always was. And that's who I still am.*

A little of the old confidence is what I was after as I made my way to the Parker House hotel. *Just a little of the old confidence!*

But when I gave my bag to a bellhop dressed like Zorro in a preposterous flowing black cape I thought I saw him sneer at me, and it made me dizzy.

It was dusk when Bradford and Woodcock came into the lobby in their coats and ties. I watched them, not the boys I'd been dreaming to life all day, but two men suddenly, entering a city the way men do, taking out their credit cards, presenting their credentials.

Together we went to Logan Airport to meet Robinson, and I walked right past him. His hair had turned completely gray. I only recognized him after he called me back.

Late the first night Robinson told us that he was losing his wife. He could feel it. "Hell," he said, "I can't even explain why. There's no *one thing;* marriage is like the environment, it can withstand a big, direct hit like the Exxon disaster, but it's the slow, steady, day by day depletion that kills it in the long run."

I listened to him and wondered if I could lose Colleen. If there would be a time up ahead of us, when our children were grown, when she would explain to them what had brought about the end of our marriage . . . "*It started when your father lost his job at Colgate. We sold our house, the house I loved, and we moved away from all our friends, and your father wouldn't spend time with us anymore after that. He spent his days at a Little League field hitting golf balls with some man. And he wouldn't accept responsibility for the things that happened, he just went around blaming the world and holding on to this ancient picture of himself as somebody who deserved an exceptional life.*"

I lay awake that first night in the hotel thinking back to the night soon after I was fired when I went around the house with a flashlight deciding which of our possessions we could sell. I began to think that someday I might visit my family in a house that was unfamiliar to me. I saw myself standing at the front door, knocking.

I had thought that we were just going to laugh all weekend, but we spent most of the time sharing a park bench quietly, the way Paul Simon's old song said we would, and I couldn't shake the dizziness. We talked a lot about our last summer together, and as I listened to my friends describing those days I recalled the old guests and their peculiar ways. Mrs. Bowman was in her nineties and still swam a mile in the ocean every morning, no matter how rough the seas. Mr. and Mrs. Waldor played their instruments in the music room every Sunday night. He played the cello and she played the violin. They had been at Auschwitz. Each time they finished playing, the hotel guests applauded and crowded softly around them, and Mr. Waldor always shook his head sadly and said, "Not so good. It was not so good, I am sorry."

I talked about an elderly woman named Mrs. Eyre whom I hadn't thought of in twenty-five years. I brought her the same breakfast every morning for two summers straight: a three-minute boiled egg, a five-ounce glass of S. S. Pierce unsweetened grapefruit juice, unbuttered whole wheat toast, cut diagonally, and a *New York Times.* She was in her nineties and she loved to talk with me on those mornings when I would arrive at her cottage riding a bellhop bicycle, balancing her breakfast on a silver tray with one hand. One morning she told me she would be going for a sunset sail with some friends and if I could get her a reliable weather report she would be most pleased. I was on the beach that afternoon when one of the lifeguards mentioned thunderstorm warnings that had been posted. I ran all the way back into town to tell Mrs. Eyre, to try and spare her some misfortune at sea. I found her sitting beside the hotel swimming pool with a group of ladies playing cards. I walked up to her table. Her back was to me, but one of the ladies gestured. "I heard the weather forecast," I said eagerly when she turned to me. The blood drained out of her face. Her jaw fell and she shook her head. "No, no," she said scornfully. "I'm entertaining now."

"I still remember the feeling of wanting to evaporate when she said this," I told my friends.

"You took it so seriously," Bradford said. "Once you were promoted to night manager or whatever it was you were, you barely spoke to the rest of us. We were beneath notice."

"What are you talking about?" I asked.

"Come on," he said. "You must remember. You had your own private table in the dining room. You wore those red pants."

Everyone laughed except me when he related the story of the time he tried to remind me who I was. Once I began taking my meals in the dining room with the guests it was his responsibility to bring me little square pats of butter and to keep my crystal water glass full. One night at dinner while I was greeting the hotel guests passing my table in their evening gowns and dinner jackets, he kept pouring water into my glass until it flooded the table and soaked my crotch. "Have a nice meal, sir," he said, throwing his head back and wheeling away across the dining room.

Suddenly I remembered all of it. How badly I had wanted to please the guests and my employers at the hotel and how, because it was the summer of 1970, this had placed me at odds with most of the other workers. There were so many people young at the same time in America, and most of them were pressing hard against the closed doors of authority that every generation leans against in its youth. Then, wham! The doors sprung off their hinges. We don't really define ourselves by our liberties, but by our limitations, and when you're young you know who you are by the boundaries placed around you. That summer when the boundaries suddenly vanished I was just plain bewildered. Twenty of the young hotel workers hid in the rosebushes along Payne Street and threw ripe tomatoes at the color guard that led the Fourth of July parade. When one of the summer policemen opened fire with live amunition and later apologized and said it had been an accident, I think I was the only person under fifty years of age who believed him. The hotel chef, a man who seemed as devoted as I was to pleasing the wealthy guests, spent two or three days each week creating magnificent ice carvings for the head table in the dining room. He would work away like a surgeon carving a bluefish or a harpoon boat out of ice. I was not part of the group that broke into the walk-in freezer and placed one of his masterpieces on the pilot light of the gas range so that it was only a snowball by morning. That summer the fragile truce that had always stood between the guests and the workers fell apart. King Chaffee was an eighty-year-old guest who tried to pull up the skirt of one of the chambermaids, a shy Russian history major at Smith College whom everyone liked. Some of the staff paid Mr. Chaffee back for his lust, filling his bed with soft-shell clams.

I remembered wanting to be a part of these pranks but wanting even more to be liked by the summer people because I knew that they were the ones who doled out the jobs and the privileges. If they liked me they could keep bad things from happening to me; most of all, they could keep me from ever slipping back into the world I was trying hard to leave behind. I held this romanticized belief that if I played scrupulously by the rules, then I would always be able to bring prizes home to my family and friends.

That night in Boston I felt that I had never moved even a few steps beyond my old fears. Never grown up at all. Bradford and I were talking after the others had fallen asleep. I kept trying to explain the way I'd behaved at the hotel. "I needed their money a lot more than you did," I said.

"Fuck you," he said with a smile. "You were just an asshole." He held out his hands and told me to throw him something. "Anything," he whispered. "Throw me the room key."

I did and it fell to the floor.

"You never could catch," I told him.

He told me that he'd just gotten his diagnosis that week, he was going to tell us all in the morning.

"I've got multiple sclerosis," he said.

He went on to say that he sometimes went through his days fantasizing about everything just coming down around him. A disaster hits, he said, and suddenly all the bets are off. There are armed bands of thugs sweeping through the cities and towns, life's become unbearable. We've all agreed in advance on a day to make our retreat. He described in detail and with some relish how I would bring my family, and Woodcock and Robinson and Big Jim would bring theirs, along the back roads of Maine to Sandy Point, the Bradford family's marvelous summer place. We would defend the piece of land, grow our own food, hold daily lessons for the children, and if things got desperate we'd have his boat, which was large enough for all of us to sail across the Atlantic. We would all be together again after so long.

"Sometimes I welcome the chance to put myself up against it all," he said.

He said sadly that when Napoleon's army had grown too large for him to know each officer, he wrote only one question next to each man's name on the list eligible for promotion — *Is he lucky?* He'd send his staff to find out if the man was a lucky man.

"We've been lucky," he said. "Healthy. Loved. You know — appreciated. Free, to a certain degree."

He told me that I had always been the luckiest.

I didn't feel lucky. I had a sick feeling in my stomach that came with the realization that I had worked my whole life to get to a place where I could be some kind of hero to my friends, and now I was wobbling on my feet just when my friend needed to lean against me.

Before he fell asleep Bradford asked me how things looked for the next school year. I lied to him. I told him that I had some good prospects and that I expected to hear something any day. He accepted this completely.

You get up too early in a hotel and you spoil all the fun. I didn't sleep at all. I spent the night wandering the hallways, and I saw the beautiful dining room hostess before she had time to put on her mascara and her padded bra. The leaves of the plants that looked so real in the lobby were being polished with Pledge, and on the table next to the house telephones there was a cigarette butt kissed by red lips and left bleeding in half a glass of ginger ale. It was before sunrise, before the illusion was restored, before the oak furnishings, the gleaming chrome, and the nautical greens declared, *You are a patrician and a stunning success, and this, my friend, is your private club.* The bellhop watched me warily. He was between acts and without his Zorro cape he looked lost and wasted, and for a moment I thought he had been waiting for me, waiting to escort me backstage to show me that everything I had always believed to be true about myself was only some kind of trick. I couldn't read his expression, couldn't tell if he was going to scream at me — *Hey, what the fuck did you expect, mister?* Or if he was going to try to warn me — *No, no, no, go back, go back to sleep, sir. It is not good that you should see everything this way. Go back, I beg you!*

I had a late bus home and after everyone left I stood at the window of our room looking down into the narrow gray streets of the city. I remembered coming to Boston once during college with a couple of fraternity brothers. We were in Harvard Square when a rally against the Vietnam War turned violent. There were cops on horseback running down students. We ended up in a girls' dormitory room at Northeastern University, and I stood at a window late that night and watched a kid walking down a side street, smashing the windshields of cars that were parked along the curb. He went from car to car, methodically smashing all the windshields. He swung so hard that his feet lifted off the ground. I remembered being scared and thinking that I didn't ever want to be on the outside of the life in America that we all believe is so good and so safe and so greatly to be desired. I was willing to do anything to be accepted inside.

Willing to do anything, I kept saying to myself as I stood at the window. *Trying to please people, trying to be liked.* I felt disgusted with myself, and in the next minute certain that my superiors and the deans at Colgate had seen this flaw in me. Maybe I had tried too hard to please my students, given too many good grades or too often crossed the line that must separate professors from their students.

I had no place to go at checkout time and so I sat in the lobby watching a different bellhop bowing and nodding deferentially to the guests he hoped would reward him with a tip. I began to feel more and more certain with each passing minute that I would never be hired as a professor again, that even while I sat in the lobby of the Parker House hotel word of my flaw was being passed along to the six remaining colleges where I had applied.

And if I had no job, no means of supporting myself, how would I ever be able to help my friends if they needed me? I thought of Bradford driving home, his fingers growing stiff on the steering wheel, the disease silent and deadly inside him. He had always been there for me since we were boys.

I just sat there feeling more and more disgusted with myself until finally I turned my mind toward what I might do next. I tried to be calm. I watched the hotel guests in their lovely business suits and I went down a checklist of people I knew in Boston who might help me find a new profession. I had a golf bag filling with rejection letters and I wasn't ever going to teach at college again, but so what, there were other professions.

Finally I remembered someone who had taught with me in a boarding school in Maine more than twenty years earlier, right after we'd finished college. We had stayed in touch and I knew that after he left teaching for a position in a publishing house in Boston he had risen through the corporate ranks to become a vice president of some department. Before I knew what I wanted to ask him, I had him on the telephone.

"God. How are you?" he exclaimed. "How are things at Colgate?"

"Fine," I told him. "Things are fine but I was just . . . in town here and wondering if I could come see you."

"Of course," he said. And he invited me for lunch.

He had on a beautiful business suit too, and we were standing in line in the cafeteria of his office building, waiting to order lunch, when his beeper went off. "Damn," he said. "I'll be right back."

"What do you want me to order for you?" I asked. But he was already leaving. I moved along in the line and I must have said something to make the kitchen worker think I had ordered the chicken à la king. When she handed it to me it looked awful but I didn't have the courage to refuse it.

I was sitting at a table surrounded by people in suits who were talking about business. I kept holding my breath while I waited for my friend to return. I felt like I was back at the summer hotel, wanting to evaporate.

At last he came back, biting into a red apple. "Lunch," he said. "I just found out I have a meeting. I'm sorry."

I started to get up and he said, "No, no, I've got a couple minutes. This is great. How are things going?"

It took a while for me to ask him for a job. I took great care to make it sound like I really didn't need a job, and that I was just thinking about the possibility of going into some other line of work. I remember telling him that with four kids now, I needed more money.

"Absolutely," he said. Then he asked me if I had time to wait for his meeting to end. "It'll be an hour, tops," he said.

It ended up being closer to two hours. The whole cafeteria emptied around me until I was left in my plastic chair feeling like a little boy in grade school. When he finally came back we talked for quite a while and he was very kind and I could tell it was hard for him to tell me that he wouldn't be able to help me. "I really don't think you'd want to work here," he said.

"Maybe you could put me out on the road, selling books," I said. "It's not a question of whether or not I could sell books, is it? Because I mean, for years I've been selling books, I mean selling *literature* to students who don't read."

He looked like he was interested, but then he said, "The truth is that the people we hire here are in their early twenties, right out of college or business school, for the most part. I couldn't even recommend you without looking silly. People would wonder what I was doing. It wouldn't make sense."

"Yes," I said, "I understand."

But I rode the bus home feeling so humiliated that I didn't see how I was going to be able to face Colleen. I kept going over what had happened, changing parts of it in my mind and trying to shake the feeling I'd had that this man knew things about me I didn't know myself.

There were plenty of times in the months that followed when all that kept me from trying to get a regular job in the real world was the memory of my friend's discomfort as we waited together for the elevator. I had told him by then that I was no longer on the faculty at Colgate and that I wasn't sure I'd ever teach again. Each time I spoke another sentence he grew more pale.

6

Final Colgate paycheck $2,082.00. Food $231.12. Gas
$34.35. Electricity $87.55. Boston trip $242.00. Cara's
birthday $61.00. Kids' bicycles $323.33. Loss on the
sale of house $1,733.00. Miscellaneous $29.00.

BALANCE *June 22: $12,191.56*

When I returned to the Little League
field and told the businessman that I felt bad about having lied
to my friends in Boston, he told me that I was a romantic and
that I needed to come up with a single thing that I wanted to
accomplish.

"Accomplish *when?*" I asked.

"Now," he said. "If not today, then next week."

I thought about it a few minutes while we hit our golf balls.
Then I told him that what I really wanted to do was get something with the money we had left before it was gone.

"Like what?" he asked.

It came to me at once. "A house," I said.

"Go for it then," he said.

"I'd have to spend all our money for a down payment," I
said, "and I wouldn't be able to meet the monthly mortgage
payments."

He smiled and said, "Listen, no court in the land is going to evict a family with four children. And believe me, the banks don't want your house on top of all the others they've been stuck with. Go find a house."

For days I thought of nothing else except reinstating Colleen and the kids in a house that was ours. I have no idea how many houses I looked at and how many realtors I met and spoke with on the telephone. And whenever I felt the air draining out of my balloon I returned to the Little League field for another pep talk. It turned out that the businessman had himself been through bankruptcy and managed to walk away with one of his two Mercedeses and his eight-bedroom house on the foreside by having his attorney draft a letter to the banks he owed nearly $900,000. "We let them know in no uncertain terms that they could accept *our* offer — which was five cents on the dollar — or I was going to commit suicide, in which case they would receive nothing. That's the way you have to play ball these days. My former partner managed to take fourteen million dollars in cash from a savings and loan in Kansas and move to Malaysia; it's nothing different than what the Mellons and the Rockefellers did at the turn of their century. The guy who thinks on his feet and who holds on to his anger has the best chance."

My search for houses only buttressed his theory that there was something wrong with the system, and not me. The real estate advertisements in the classified pages were right alongside the advertisements for three different diet and weight loss programs. Systems, is what they are called now, *weight loss systems.* Of course, what good is a home if you're not thin inside it, if it makes you feel fat. And on the same page of the newspaper someone was selling a size fourteen wedding dress. *Never worn,* the ad said. *Got too fat,* I guessed.

I spent hours looking through the ads each day, searching for what appeared to be an honest real estate agent. One who might say, *Hello, I'm Kelly, and I'm selling this same lovely three-bedroom ranch for the tenth time in the last five years because everyone who's bought it eventually hates the smell that comes up from the basement when it rains . . . What a fixer-upper! Earn your sweat equity by refurbishing this lovely sun-filled saltbox with a full basement and a lunatic who drives by every night at midnight in a black Mustang with his stereo blaring because his old motorcycle girlfriend used to live here. Some nights he stops his car and sets up a little shrine to the memory of this girl, right on your front lawn.*

You learn pretty quickly that most houses are not sold for happy reasons and so when you go to buy one, you are buying a measure of someone else's sorrow. I guess this is the reason for so much subterfuge in the real estate business. There is always something to hide about a house. But you have to admire the indomitable spirit of some of the real estate salespeople. There was this one advertisement that showed a picture of the salesman in midair. His smile curved up to the ends of his moustache and beneath the picture it said, "IT MAKES ME HAPPY TO MAKE YOU HAPPY!"

It was brilliant. In his simplicity he had tapped into the central belief that so many of us hold on to stubbornly. The belief that comprises the trusting embrace of Western civilization. The belief that the possession of a thing will bring happiness. I embraced it as much as the next fellow, and I suppose the real estate lady saw it in my eyes the first moment when she shook my hand. I had heard that life could be cheap on one of the islands in Casco Bay, so we hired a baby-sitter for the day and took the ferry out to look at property with the real estate lady who we'd never laid eyes on before. I had my doubts right away when she turned out to be the lady in the bright orange short-shorts and a matching orange top with *Sunworshipper* emblazoned across her bosom. Whenever I glanced up without thinking I expected it was going to say *Party Animal* on her shirt.

She drove us around the island, Colleen in the front seat next to her, me in back. We passed a man walking with a little girl, and she zapped down her window and called out, "She gets more beautiful every day, Lester." Then she zapped the window back up, punched the gas pedal, and said to Colleen, "Doesn't it amaze you how ugly women can have such beautiful children? That little girl's mother is the ugliest woman on the island."

She showed us a piece of land near a beautiful boatyard. We walked behind her as she pointed out the trees. "These are worth a lot of money," she said. "Take a look at those pines. Those are virgin! And clear! There won't be many knots in them at all and you can hire a fellow with a portable saw mill who will cut them down and mill for you right on the land. I bet you could build practically your whole house out of them." She reached out and ran her red fingernails along the bark of one tree. "Gosh," she exclaimed, "these are such great trees, it makes me want to buy the property myself just to cut them down."

Maybe property wasn't the answer for us, I said. Maybe we should look at a house or two.

A shack owned by a local lobsterman was for sale for $169,000. Inside, two of the man's sons were slouched on a couch, watching television in the middle of the day. I stood with them while Colleen followed the lady from room to room. There was a man cooking on the TV. "You guys interested in learning how to cook?" I asked the boys. They shrugged. I pointed to some small islands outside the window. "You know what those islands are?" I asked. They shook their heads and shrugged again. Before we'd left for the ferry that morning I had eaten my Cheerios with Erin and told her that we might live on an island. "Maybe we'll buy an old lobster boat," I said dreamily. "We'll fix it up and turn it into a grocery boat, and you and your sisters and Jack and I will get up early and go to the mainland for food and then we'll bring it to the people who live on the island."

"How will we know what they want?"

"Well, they'll call us the night before and we'll take their orders. Then in the morning we'll go pick up what everybody needs."

"Wow," she said.

Now I washed up onto the rocks with the prospect of her going out on dates with island boys who watched cooking shows on TV in the middle of bright summer days. This was precisely the Maine life I had worked so hard to escape.

Back inside her car the lady told us the lobsterman had built the place himself for sixteen thousand dollars and had to sell it now because he couldn't pay the taxes, which had risen to nearly four thousand a year. "He'll be a rich man when he sells," she said happily. "Of course he'll blow it all on booze, he's a terrible drunk. A nice enough guy if you're not married to him, I guess."

She had to drive to her house for a few minutes, she told us. She was in the middle of a personal transaction, applying for a home equity loan, and the bank had sent someone to the island early that morning to appraise her house.

When we got there she had a brief conversation with the appraiser while Colleen and I sat out on her deck with the potted geraniums and a beautiful view of Casco Bay and the Portland skyline. After a few minutes we heard her yelling in the kitchen. "Look, you'd better not low-ball this place, that's all I can say.

You call it a chalet, but let me tell you something, the tile on this floor came from Italy, and look at these windows, they're *better* than Anderson windows!"

She ended up showing us one more house before she dumped us off at the dock. It was a handsome white clapboard farmhouse with black shutters. An elderly woman lived there alone, and though it wasn't officially "on the market" the real estate lady had the inside track with the woman's two sons, who were planning to pack up their mother in the fall and put her in a nursing home in New Jersey.

It happened again. I looked up and expected to see *Party Animal*. She stood with her feet apart, a clipboard in one hand, her legs tanned to a shoepolish brown. I took a long look at her as the ferry pulled away from the dock and I felt myself leaning back again and feeling like I was seeing America for the first time. I mean, what America had become while I'd been plowing ahead with my head down, filling my pockets along the way.

I watched as she climbed into her car and drove up the hill to her next appointment. She stopped once and waved to a lobsterman who was pulling up to the pier. I wondered if this was the man who owned the shack we'd walked through, if this was the boys' father. I watched him walk along the deck of his boat and I wanted to know what it meant when a man builds a house for sixteen thousand bucks and the years pass and then a lady in orange short-shorts tells him his house is worth ten times this much, and she knows because she's sold the houses and property of everyone the fisherman has ever known; some of the houses that he used to walk by every day of his life she has sold five or six times for enormous piles of money — money that doesn't seem real to him compared to the land and the buildings he's known for so many years. And if his house is worth ten times what *he knows* it's worth because a lady with *Party Animal* written across her chest tells him this, then what is a day of his work worth? And what is his marriage worth? And what's it worth to spend an afternoon teaching his sons the names of the islands beyond their window?

In this one afternoon I saw it all — the life I had run from, and the life I was running toward. The low bass note of poverty, and the screeching high of prosperity. All that was required of a man in order to find his place at some sensible point between these two extremes was judgment, the moderating influence of reason. I wondered if this was something I did not possess, if I had given it up in my effort to be liked and to get ahead or lost it somewhere along the way in my rush forward.

That night Colleen was sitting up with Erin when I came back from my walk. I went into Jack's room and picked him up in his sleep to take him to the bathroom to pee so he wouldn't wet his bed. I carried him into the living room and showed him to Colleen and Erin. "Isn't he handsome," I said. Then I watched Erin looking at him. She couldn't keep from smiling at her brother, and then patting his cheeks, and finally kissing this boy who tormented her all day long when he was awake.

After I put Jack back in his bed I went downstairs into the living room and turned on the radio to catch the score of the Red Sox game. An old song by Donovan came on and I started singing it out loud. When I saw Erin smiling, I just started getting into it, singing louder and then bebopping across the living room floor until I was outside myself. "Hey, look at this new dance!" I shouted above the music. "The real estate dance!" I turned myself into a knock-kneed chicken-winged fool, grinding and shaking and squawking the lyrics while holding my hands out for money and then pulling out the lining of all my pockets. Erin was laughing and trying to dance along with me. "Take a look at this *view!*" I screamed. "What would this view do for *you?* Put you in debt 'till you turn *blue!* What else are you gonna *do!*"

I knew I was riding the edge of absurdity but I kept going, changing into a slower song now to the tune of "On the Street Where You Live," from *My Fair Lady*. "There are lawyers now, in this part of town. And they've—" When I looked into Colleen's eyes I saw that she was crying.

"What's wrong?" I asked her.

"You sound so awful," she said.

"I was just trying to make everyone laugh," I said, turning off the radio. "I'm sorry."

"It isn't funny," she said. "It scared me. You can't see yourself, but we can, and we're all scared."

I felt like hell about this, and I told the businessman that I was dropping out of the housing market. "There's only money flowing out now," I said woefully, "every day our bank balance gets a little smaller."

He told me that I was too sensitive. "Look, here's a better idea," he said. "Take whatever money you have and send it to a friend to keep for you, then apply for all the credit cards you can. When they ask you what your income is, just put down any six-figure number. Max the cards out on cash advances for your down payment. Man, you've got to come up with some anger. What you need to survive out there is anger and *plastic*. One month after you buy the house you send a letter to the credit card companies explaining that you've lost your job, you're broke, and if they push you for their money you'll be in bankruptcy before they can get back from lunch. Buy yourself an answering machine too if you don't already have one so you can screen the calls from the collection agencies. And they *will* call, believe me. They're the only people who work Christmas morning and Easter Sunday. But remember, time is on your side; we don't have a debtor's prison in this country. And remember this too, credit card companies are run by banks, and by some of the most arrogant and cynical people you could ever want to meet. Do you know that they market themselves to the poor? Sure, because the poor need the plastic and they take a long time paying off their balance. That's a ton of interest for the bank, my friend. As a matter of fact, 'deadbeats' in their business are the guys who pay their balances off every month. That's right, they call them 'deadbeats.' Now, tell me, is that the height of cynicism or what? You — my friend — need anger in your belly!"

On my way home from the Little League field one day the next week I stopped at the pharmacy in the Shop & Save to pick up a bottle of Benadryl because we had four children at home with chicken pox. We had turned the big bedroom on the second floor into an army field hospital where we dispensed the Benadryl and Popsicles on demand and took turns giving the kids oatmeal baths. We sewed mittens to the cuffs of Cara's and Jack's pajama shirts so they wouldn't scratch off the scabs in their tormented sleep. I couldn't bear to see their eyes swollen and their scalps covered with sores.

I was waiting in line at the pharmacy when a short, pale-faced man in army fatigues and boots standing next to me held up his bottle and said, "Chicken pox?"

We got to talking. "I'd like to be home, helping the wife," he said. "But I've got too much work to do."

"What kind of work?" I asked him.

"I've got my own company," he said.

I was thinking in slightly grander terms than Jiffy Clean, the company name advertised in big blue letters emblazoned across both sides of his van. He had parked right beside me, and before we drove off he told me that he had been in business three years. "The only bad part is the hours," he explained. "I usually go ten hours every day, then go home, eat supper, and sleep for five hours, then work all night on the office buildings. What about you?"

"Well," I said, "I'm out of work right now." Before I could dazzle him with my employment history, he skipped over to me and handed me a business card.

"I've got a bid in for a big law firm," he said merrily. "If I get it, I could use you. We don't do windows, but like I said, the hours are long."

I took his card, thanked him, and stood there in silence for a few seconds before the anger kicked in and I began saying under my breath — *Do I look like a fucking janitor to you, pal? No offense, but I don't think the JIFFY CLEAN company is in my future. I'm a college professor. Can't you tell by looking at me?*

7

I remember the angry days best, maybe because I put so much effort into convincing myself that I had a right to be pissed off. I had summoned a small degree of anger during my final days at Colgate, but this new anger was far more satisfying because it was undefined, wild, and inspiring. When I was an adolescent I didn't behave like one because I was already working too hard at being liked and getting ahead. I was behaving like one now and it made me feel that I was finally evening the score.

One morning all four kids were crying miserably. I couldn't appease them with offers of any kind — a Batman comic book for Jack, a bottle for Cara, books and clay for Erin and Nellie. I was standing in the middle of the bedroom hanging my head in defeat when Colleen came up the stairs. She took over without hesitation, undressing each of them. "Go start the bath, please," she said to me. I did. And when I returned I found the kids all naked doing ballet lessons together.

I went down to the kitchen, already angry about my wife's extreme competence, where I heard Alex Chadwick on National Public Radio saying, "Professor W—— joins us now from Colgate University in upstate New York." As soon as I heard Professor W——'s voice I felt like I wanted to break something with my bare hands. He began droning on in a lifeless explanation of recent stock market gains. I heard the arrogance in his voice and it seemed like just the other day when I had run into him at Colgate University. It was our first year there and we were sky-high about the place. On a Sunday morning Colleen and I took the kids to the magnificent stone field house to burn off some energy. As we passed behind one of the tennis courts a man stopped me and told me we were making too much noise. I'd been watching him in his tennis outfit with striped wristbands that matched the stripes on his socks. He was being hammered by a man with one short leg. "People don't bring children into the field house," he said to me. He had a frown on his face and it stayed there while he spoke. I wanted my mind to go slowly over this, and to come to some understanding of what was taking place before I said anything.

"Are you on the faculty?" he asked, still frowning. "These facilities are reserved for the faculty in the morning."

I looked at his frown, then into his brown eyes.

"Are you on the faculty?" he asked me a second time.

I was too dumbfounded to speak.

He said again, "These courts are for faculty members."

I heard Colleen calling to me from the track that ringed the tennis courts. Her voice was trying to slow my mind down too, I could tell. I was too frightened to defend myself. I was still the new kid on the block, the kid who was going to have to make no enemies until after he was granted tenure.

A month later, Colleen and I were having dinner at the president's house. I looked up from my shrimp cocktail and saw the man from the tennis courts sitting across from me. He was a professor in the economics department, and would soon be named to the dean of faculty's council and would advise the dean on matters of tenure and promotion. We had already bought the house on Maple Avenue and were setting our sights on a fourth baby.

Most of the day I let the anger wash through me while I thought about what I could do to him. I was cutting kindling for the woodstove when it came to me. I called Professor W——— at Colgate and reached him in his office.

"Professor, this is Scott Simon at National Public Radio. We've had numerous calls here today about your interview this morning. Most of them from your colleagues around the country."

"I see."

"Yes, and I wonder if we might pass along your telephone number to professors who call in, wishing to speak with you."

"Yes, that would be fine," he replied.

I thanked him.

The telephone was still warm in my hand when I called Professor W——— at his home. "This is Stanley Peterson in the economics department at Tufts University. Look, I heard you on NPR this morning and I just wanted to ask how in God's name you ever got through graduate school!"

I called three more times that afternoon and it was just before midnight when I called him with a Texas accent. "Professor

W——? This is Professor Drysdale from Austin calling. Man you are full of cow shit, you know that?"

The anger came more and more easily after that. One day when Colleen was sitting in the kitchen feeding Cara I took the telephone call at the counter from a collection agency that had tracked us down and was trying to collect a heating oil bill we had left behind. "Our records show that you promised to pay this by the end of the month, Mr. Snyder."

"No, I never promised that," I said. "I ordered fifty gallons of oil to get us through our last month in the house; it's not my fault the truck delivered two hundred."

"The oil was delivered to your residence, Mr. Snyder."

"I didn't ask for two hundred gallons of oil."

"We've spoken to your wife on several occasions."

"Oh yeah? We'll you're speaking to me now and I don't want you calling my wife again."

"So, what should we do then, Mr. Snyder?"

"Send the bill back to the oil company."

"We don't submit bills here, Mr. Snyder."

"I'll submit it myself."

"It's too late for that, Mr. Snyder. So you're telling me you're going to break your promise to pay this by the end of the month, Mr. Snyder?"

"Why do you use my name in every sentence?"

"Excuse me, Mr. Snyder?"

"I said, why do you use my name in every sentence?"

"So you don't forget that we know who you are, Mr. Snyder."

"I know who *you* are too, and I'm going to hang up the phone."

"I wouldn't do that, Mr. Snyder. This is a collection agency, doesn't that mean anything to you, Mr. Snyder?"

"Is that a rhetorical question or do you want an answer?"

"Doesn't that mean anything to you, Mr. Snyder?"

"Do you want the truth?"

"Yes, Mr. Snyder."

"The truth is, no, it doesn't mean a fucking thing to me. Not a goddamned fucking thing."

"Thank you, Mr. Snyder. Have a nice day now."

The next time I went to the Little League field I told the businessman about this.

"Did you get the credit cards?" he asked.

I told him I hadn't. "I didn't think I could lie about my income."

"You're just lying to a computer, that's all," he said. He had grown impatient with me. "This country's finished, friend. The signs are everywhere. AT&T lays off forty thousand workers and its stock goes up! Do you know what this means?" His voice was shaky. There was a wild look in his eyes. "It means the covenant has been broken."

He told me about another business associate of his who had recently taught a course at Dartmouth, in the Amos Tuck School. "He had this brilliant black kid from the projects in the South Bronx. At graduation my friend was standing with the boy's father and he asked the man how bad things were in the city. The father said, 'Professor, one of these days you're going to be able to see the flames from here.'"

We walked into the woods and began searching for my ball. "Most guys my age don't get it," he said bitterly. "We've created a whole class of people, an underclass that's getting bigger and bigger and more and more disenfranchised from the good stuff that this country offers. They're in the cities right now just working themselves into a frenzy. A buddy of mine is a cop in Milwaukee—*Milwaukee*, for Christ's sake! He tells me that there's a whole subculture of predators, real mean guys who are going to make us pay someday. There's going to be hell to pay because they're going to come screaming into the suburbs of this country, right up to the first tee at the country club, and they're going to point their guns at us and say, 'ANTE UP, YOU FAT MOTHERFUCKERS! YOU'VE HAD IT TOO GOOD FOR TOO LONG!' "

His face turned pink and I could see the tiny blood vessels in his cheeks.

"We can forget the ball," I said. "I'll buy some new ones."

"No, no," he said. "Ever since I stopped earning money, I never walk away from a lost ball. These babies cost more than a buck apiece."

I practically quoted him a few days later when my father telephoned me from Pennsylvania. As soon as I heard his voice I knew that something was wrong. He described how a man had come into their apartment in broad daylight and stolen my stepmother's pocketbook off the couch in the living room. "We were right in the next room," he said. "Can you imagine?"

My father was a retired minister, living on a small pension. He had lived his whole life without ever throwing a fist in anger. Now he was scared and I was too far away to protect him. I felt awful about this, and as I listened to him I remembered that the last time we had spoken I had a job and a house in a safe place and what seemed like a guarantee that I would always be able to satisfy the only thing my father had ever asked of me, that I not let him and my stepmother be separated when they could no longer care for themselves. As a pastor he had seen this happen to old married couples and he considered it the cruelest thing that could be imagined.

"The people are coming out of the cities and doing these awful things!" he yelled into the telephone. Then he went on speaking in a loud, frantic voice about how the country was going down the drain because the government had outlawed school prayer and sanctioned abortions and taxed the middle class and paid welfare mothers to have babies out of wedlock. I'd never heard him speak that way and I'd never heard him so angry. "I lost two buddies in the war," he shouted at me. "Charlie Blackledge died at Normandy, and Ralph Blake was shot down over Africa, and for what! What did those boys die for?"

I tried to interrupt him but he kept going. "The taxes — where does all that money go!"

"Hold on!" I shouted. "You don't pay any taxes!"

"I won't hold on! I'll tell you right now — Hillary Clinton is running the whole thing, and she's —"

"Hey, Dad, love it or leave it!" I yelled at him. I remembered him saying this to me once in the late 1960s when he heard me making fun of President Nixon. I said it again, "Love it or leave it, Dad. Remember?"

I hung up on him, the first time I'd ever done that. I left the house and started running up the sidewalk to the main road. At the intersection I turned right and ran for five miles to Falmouth, thinking the whole time about how my father had worked to support me. I remembered him taking a night shift job one winter washing out the inside of milk trucks, and another job loading freight on trucks. If he had been in my spot, his last paycheck gone, he would have taken any kind of job no matter what it paid or how it humbled him, just to keep going.

In Falmouth I ran past some of the most expensive houses in Maine. They stood on gently sloping lawns along a wide tree-lined street and faced the ocean. I ran by nannies out pushing their carriage babies, and joggers, their arms moving as precisely as the hands of a clock, their bodies so hard and thin I couldn't tell if they were men or women. Cars passed me, a few drivers talking on their telephones. I kept running, thinking how much I had always wanted to be able to take care of my father and how often I had told him that when push came to shove I would be *there* for him. I wondered if he had known all along that I lacked something essential, some inner strength or self-reliance, and that at the last count I was a coward. I came to the old beach road we had driven down on one of the first days back in Maine, where the cop was on duty to keep the public out. I remembered when anyone was allowed access to this beach and I wondered who the new owners were who had hired the cop to keep people like me out. What were they afraid of? I wondered.

It came into my head to go talk to the cop. I was out of my mind to think that he would be eager to speak with me, but I thought maybe we could say hello and and he might tell me who the family was that employed him to watch over their fabulous life. When I got near the cottage I slowed down. Hell, I thought, someone like this who worked for a rich person would see right away that I was out of work and drifting through my days. There was that, and also my realization as I drew nearer that his hand was reaching for his fluorescent yellow pistol.

Then it hit me. *A fluorescent yellow gun?* A few more steps and I saw that it was a water pistol and that he was an inflatable man, a life-sized dummy, perfectly dressed in a policeman's uniform probably appropriated from some long-forgotten summer stock production of *Arsenic and Old Lace*.

I started laughing and then the anger returned. I walked back along the main road, searching the sidewalk for something sharp enough to pop the dummy. All I found was a Bic pen, and when I stood face to face with the inflated cop I lost my nerve and walked away. When I got home I took the checkbook from the pocket of Colleen's coat that was hanging over a chair in the kitchen. I walked outside to the barn and went over the numbers, hoping to find that either Colleen or I had subtracted wrong. I wrote the figures down in columns on the back of a cardboard box that held the badminton set. The money was disappearing, but just writing down the numbers calmed me, and when I looked at them I felt the satisfaction that accountants must feel when they distill the complex inner yearnings of men and the forces of technology down to numbers. When I looked up, there was a beautiful sunset, a deep orange light seeping through the stand of cedar trees and dragging their long shadows across the meadow. I turned the badminton box over in my lap and gazed at a happy American family, mom, dad, son, and daughter engaged in a friendly game of badminton. The whole thing was such an obvious fabrication that it should have made me laugh, but I studied the photograph with a mounting rage. Here was a son who would take care of his father when he grew old. Here was a husband who didn't make his wife cry. The laces on all four pairs of sneakers were tied with identical bows; I pictured some employee with a salary and benefits down on his knees tying everyone's shoes. The numbers of my budget were still swimming in my head. At a cost of living of just about two thousand a month we could last until the end of December. Half a year. Then I held up the box and kicked my foot through it. *There,* I thought, looking at the torn faces, *welcome to the real world.*

When I told the businessman about this, instead of applauding my anger, he got a concerned look on his face and told me about a men's encounter group he attended in Portland one night a week. They met in a church basement and the point of the gathering was to learn not to judge yourself so harshly. As soon as he invited me to come along with him I knew I wouldn't return again to the Little League field.

"We're meeting Wednesday night this week," he said. "I can swing by and pick you up?"

"Maybe next week," I said weakly. He looked at me for a few seconds, and then when he got into position over his golf ball, before he swung, he told me he thought I should get a good life insurance policy so that my family would have something in the event anything happened to me.

"The stress," he said, not looking at me, "it's a real *killer,* you know?"

I persuaded myself that he was right, and that a $200,000 life insurance policy would provide Colleen with enough cash for a house if I dropped dead.

The trouble was that, being a smoker, I was going to have to pay twice the annual premium paid by a nonsmoker. So I lied to the insurance man, boasting of my grandparents' longevity and my robust health and swearing that I did not smoke.

I called Colleen's mother, who is a nurse, to ask her advice.

"These guys aren't dummies," she said, "they send someone to your house to take your blood and urine. The nicotine will show up."

The night before the laboratory technician came to take my blood and urine, I was still trying to figure out some way to beat the insurance company. I watched a baseball game on TV with Jack, and when I sent him off to bed with the standard instructions to brush his teeth and do a long pee, it hit me.

I held the baby food jar while Jack aimed. "Why am I peeing in this jar, Daddy?"

"It's a trick," I said.

His eyes opened wide. "A magic trick?"

"Yeah, sort of."

When he finished and nothing had happened, he was disappointed. "What's the magic, Daddy?"

I looked at him in his blue pin-striped pajamas. Then I picked him up and hugged him. "The magic is you'll still have food and sneakers if I kick the bucket."

The lab technician was a meticulously groomed fellow with no interest in small talk. He needed a table, he said. We went into the dining room and I watched him set two pairs of eyeglasses, a plastic cup, and a syringe kit in front of him and then make some small adjustments so that they were in a perfectly straight row. He had forms in triplicate and more questions about my health. I gave the right answers and when he handed me the cup for my urine I went into the bathroom and locked the door behind me. I had my son's piss in the baby food jar, submerged in warm water inside a *Beauty and the Beast* thermos.

"How many of these do you do a day?" I asked, hoping to distract him when I returned to the dining room and set the plastic cup on the table. I don't recall if he answered me. I watched him dip a thin strip of paper into the urine. "Do you have children?" he asked. *Oh Christ,* I thought, *he's got me!*

But a week later the lab results were in, and the policy was mine, and there was a day or two after that when I began to feel that perhaps the secret to surviving in the margins of our society was to be clever, not angry. I felt no guilt at all for cheating the insurance company. In fact it felt like a kind of vindication when, shortly after getting the policy, a perfect job opened up at Princeton University. I put the notice from the *Chronicle of Higher Education* on the refrigerator door beneath the kids' magnetic letters and walked around rehearsing my explanation of why I'd been fired like an accused man going over his alibi before the police question him. My mind kept enlarging how great it was going to be for us to settle in that beautiful town and how Colleen and I would ride the train into Manhattan to see the museums and the Broadway shows.

"I can't wait to show you the place," I told Colleen one night when she was lying in my arms. A band of moonlight was ironed across our bed. I turned my head and watched the night breeze fill the lace curtains. "Maybe we should take a family trip to Princeton," I said.

"When will they interview candidates?"

"A couple weeks, probably."

"Maybe we should wait then. We could all go with you to the interview."

I was blind with excitement. Blind to Colleen's reluctance to grab hold of this possibility. She saw it for what it was, an advertisement in a journal, to which several hundred if not thousands of jobless people would apply if for no other reason than to get the health insurance benefits. I saw it as the perfect next step in my career. When you climb the ladder high enough, a job at Princeton is one of the things you see out there against the horizon. The mere listing of this job ratified my prediction that a better job was out there and my long-held belief that hard work and persistence *entitled* me to have it.

I sent out a résumé and cover letter and then started spending time again with my family. On the beach one day we were building a sand castle together when Erin said, "Let's build a little town instead. Let's build Hamilton. We can put our house right here, and our school right there, and the supermarket—"

I interrupted. "Wait a minute. If we're going to build a town, let's build Princeton, New Jersey. Let's see, why don't we put our new house right here."

"Have you lived there before, Daddy?" Nell asked as she dug in.

I confessed that I'd never seen the place.

"Where's Brian Murphy's house in *Princeland!*" Jack hollered.

"It's *Princeton!*" Erin told him.

Later I placed an imposter's telephone call to the English department. "Yeah, my name's Terrance Delmonico. How are you today, sir? I'm an alum, class of fifty-nine. I'm going to recommend somebody to you for the vacancy in the department that you've advertised. I'm just wondering, when do you plan to issue invitations for interviews?"

Another ten days. I remember hanging up the telephone and then staring at it for a few seconds, first wondering what the hell I was going to do with all the days between now and the time I had my interview, and then asking myself one more question — *Is a guy entitled to a job at Princeton who does shit like faking phone calls and cheating insurance companies?*

I found my answer on the evening news every time there was another story about layoffs and buyouts and corporate greed. I had played by the rules for years, but there weren't any more rules. Just like the businessman had said. In the new age, those entitled to the prizes were those who learned how to break the rules and get away with it. Or maybe it had always been that way and I just never saw it.

8

Food $233.00. Telephone $43.55. Car insurance
$229.77. Golf balls $4.24. Gas for car $22.00.
Miscellaneous $125.00.

B A L A N C E *July 4: $11,534.00*

Colleen and I were sitting on the bridge
over the Royal River watching the Fourth of July fireworks in the
sky above Casco Bay when she told me that I needed to be more
careful about swearing in front of the kids. I apologized. "Because
I've noticed that your language has gotten pretty bad," she said.

"I said I was sorry."

The kids were in our arms, in their striped summer pajamas,
their cheeks sunburned and their blond hair still wet from their
evening bath. We were one big happy family to the passing cars. I
leaned over Jack and kissed the top of his head. I hadn't known
anything at all about babies until Colleen taught me, and I was
thinking about the time she explained the soft spot on Erin's head
where the skull was still forming.

"If I tell you about the IRS will you swear at me?" she asked.

I felt at once like the bridge had begun swaying underneath us.
"What is it?" I asked her.

103

"You didn't figure the tax right."

"What tax?"

"On the money from your pension. The IRS wrote. I didn't want you to see the letter."

"Why not? How much more do they want?"

"I paid them."

"How much?"

"Three thousand."

I pressed my lips against the top of Jack's head, waiting to catch my breath. *Lousy fuckers!* I thought.

I heard Colleen say, "I wish we could just be happy and not want anything that we don't already have."

"Like what?" I said miserably.

"Like the job at Princeton, or any other job."

"If I don't get that job, what do we have to be happy about?"

She didn't answer. I watched as she pulled the children close to her.

In the mail that first week in July there was a form letter from another college telling me how much they had enjoyed reading my application materials but that they had selected another candidate. What made this rejection different from the others was that it was a small college marooned on an outpost of northern Michigan where, one suspected, the principal winter sport was ice fishing. I thought I'd get the job hands down, and secretly I had been carrying it in my head as the job offer I would happily turn down in favor of something much better.

I decided to call one morning and ask why I hadn't been granted an interview. I got a tape telling me to call back after eight A.M. I tried a second time and got the same tape. "It's nine-thirty, you lousy fuckers!" I said to the recorded voice.

"What?" Erin asked as she passed me.

I had forgotten that it was Sunday.

I was breathing in quick shallow gasps when I finally reached the college the next day and was passed along to the chair of the English department. He recognized my name and listened patiently while I went over my seven years of college teaching at two of the finest private universities in the nation, and my three published books and the prestigious foundation grants. What I expected him to say was that I was overqualified for the job. Then he explained the situation. "When we put this advertisement in the newspapers and journals we never expected to attract anyone with your qualifications. But the truth is, we got over three hundred applications and there were nine candidates whose experience exceeded yours. One had been nominated for a Pulitzer Prize. Three were former department heads. It's just so difficult. I'm terribly sorry."

I was sitting with the telephone receiver on my knee, just staring into space when Erin came back into the room.

"Can I ask you one thing, Daddy?" she said.

"Go ahead," I said.

"Why were you fired?"

"Why was I *fired? Jesus!*" I said before I caught myself. I looked at my seven-year-old-daughter in one of those isolated time frames where you suddenly see your child grown. Only this time I saw her crippled by her father's failures and inadequacies. I saw her in middle age, her eyes the same indescribable green of her grandmother's. I saw her living alone with a cat. Sitting at a window looking out at a rainy day, and watching people pass in the normal flow of the living. They are smiling, a part of life, and she wonders how they can be so happy. And in moments of her deepest reflection she thinks back to the end of her first year of school, when she was moved from her little school into a long period of weariness that never went away completely. She is still pretty and her hands are her baby hands, pudgy so that with her fingers spread they resemble starfish.

"Well, it's a pretty long story, ducky," I told her. She was looking down at a length of yarn that she kept wrapping and unwrapping around her hand. I thought how easy it had been to have our babies. One, two, three, four, in six and a half years. Effortless. Each of them brilliantly beautiful in the delivery room. Pink skin and piercing blue or green eyes that opened wide at the sound of Colleen's voice, each of them just appearing as if summoned. None of our babies were real to me until the moment of their birth. And in the delivery room while Colleen suffered sweetly I just stood there like a stranger who had wandered in off the street to the bedside of a self-possessed young woman.

"You know," I said to Erin, "we should take one of your books and go lie under a tree and read the whole thing. Read all day. What do you say?"

She had other plans. And I admit that I was relieved. I had never been a father to sit around with his children. From the day we first brought them home I wrapped them up for long hikes, bicycle rides, cross-country skiing, skating. I had to keep busy with them because the prospect of a whole day of just being on the living room floor with them, the way Colleen had been for seven years, made me uneasy. I didn't know why. When Erin was first born I had rigged up a sling so that I could play tennis and squash with her tied to my chest. Anything to keep moving.

"Do you worry about us because I was fired?" I asked her.

"Yes," she said. "Because we might be poor."

"We won't be poor," I said.

"We don't have a house."

"Look *around,* this is a house."

"I mean a house we don't have to move from."

"We'll find a nice place to live. Even nicer than here. You like it here, don't you? You get to go to the beach every day with Mommy. You see your cousins, and Nanny and Papa?"

When I looked at her sad face I realized that I wasn't going to persuade her of anything. Whatever she felt was deep in her, already fitted in her appraisal of the world.

"I'll be Mr. Badminton again soon," I told her.

She smiled. "Who?"

"Mr. Badminton. I'll go off to work each morning the way I bet he does and we'll be the Badminton family again and everything will be all right. Mommy will be Mrs. Badminton and I'll be Mr. Badminton, and you'll be the Badminton daughter and everyone will look at us and think how lucky we are just to be the Badminton family and to live in the Badminton house."

Her smile disappeared and she gave me a look of caution, then said there wasn't any such thing as the Badminton family. I lifted her up into my arms and took her out to the barn and showed her the cardboard box with the hole I had kicked through the family's faces. "What happened?" Erin asked with alarm.

"They had a little accident," I said. "Things don't go right for a family all the time. Even for the Badminton family." I found some electrical tape and when I'd finished repairing the box I nailed it to the wall above the workbench. "That will give me something to shoot for," I said.

"You're going to *shoot* them?" Erin said, even more alarmed.

"No, no," I said, "come on, let's go get an ice-cream cone."

We walked to town and back. I wanted to tell her something that would make sense to her. At the top of the hill I told her to look up into the sky. "We don't know how far it goes," I said. "We don't even know that. People pretend to know the answers to things, but really all we know is that we pop out of somebody's belly like you popped out of Mommy, and then we try to live and to be happy. And sometimes we get lost. We get fired and we move away from friends and then we aren't happy for a while, maybe for a long time. But then we *are* happy again. And there's a big difference between being poor and being broke."

"Broke?" she asked. "You mean the way the Badminton family was broken on the box?"

I laughed and told her yes, that was just what I meant.

"And you mean the way the car is broken?"

"The car's not broken, sweetie."

"It was when Mommy was driving it this morning. Lots of smoke was coming out of it."

Dave, the mechanic, estimated that it would cost around twelve hundred dollars to replace the rear axle and wheel bearings, and after finding leaks in the radiator and the brake line, he didn't think a car with 113,000 miles on it was worth this kind of repair.

I think if I had even the smallest belief that I was actually going to land the Princeton job, I would not have called my former student in Ohio whose father owned the Ford dealership. On the telephone I told her I needed her help because without a job I wasn't going to be able to qualify for a bank loan. She assured me that she could do "in-house financing," and she said she was glad to be able to help.

I expected to drive back from Ohio in my new station wagon (a Ford Taurus with the third seat in back is what I was hoping for), but since round-trip plane fare was considerably less than the price of two one-way tickets, I booked round-trip.

I am not a man who ever found it easy to pick up women, and I have never considered myself a ladies man. The only time a woman ever propositioned me was in Hollywood after a book I'd written had been sold to Paramount Pictures. I found myself in a suite in the Beverly Wilshire Hotel for four days with the head of the small production company working with Paramount on the project picking me up in a limousine and taking me to meetings and dinners. That is where it would have happened, in the backseat, but I had recently met and fallen in love with Colleen and to me it would have felt like betrayal. Years later another member of the production company told me if I had shut my eyes and enjoyed myself for ten minutes the movie project wouldn't have been dumped.

So, I lied to Colleen this time and told her I had been invited to the campus of a small nonexistent college in Ohio to which I gave the name Langdon College.

It's surprising how, living in the midst of change the way we do, we find from time to time that some things have remained the way they always were. Flying in the middle of the week on a plane from Boston to Ohio nearly all my fellow travelers in business suits were still white (very white and pale-faced) men. At the moment we all dropped our tray stands to be served lunch, we looked like a kindergarten class of overgrown little boys in high chairs. Some of us even opened the napkins and tucked them into our shirt collars so they hung just below our chins exactly the way our mothers had taught us when we first took our place at the dinner table. Some wore suspenders like I was ordered to wear as a kid. Most all of us had been cared for and taught our most fundamental skills by women. Where were these women now, I wondered. *Exactly where* were they? In nursing homes? The lucky ones maybe in Florida inching along golf courses and sitting in doctors' waiting rooms. What would they say if they were to discover that after all their sacrifices and work, all their coddling and their lectures, these boys had grown up to become men who unzipped their pants and climbed on top of women that were not their wives. I looked around carefully and wondered how many of my confederates had coloring in their hair, false teeth, toupees, lifts in their shoes, antacid tablets in their toilet kits. A woman's vanity, it seems to me, is honest, for it is tied almost always to her need to attract. But a man's is tied to his ambition and therefore never to be trusted.

I wondered who among us in the airplane, when he day-dreamed about sex, still pictured his wife. It made me think how when I had first known Colleen I had stared into her eyes when I made love to her. Like I was worshiping her. I had always felt such gratitude. So, I thought, if I cheated on her would I ever be able to look into her eyes like that again? Well . . . Maybe if I cheated on her my feeling of gratitude would be revived. I would be over-whelmed with gratitude for her long suffering. The man beside me looked up suddenly from his laptop computer and stared off into space as if beyond the loud hissing of the plane's pressurized cabin he had heard a voice calling his name. Heard it distinctly, like his mother's voice calling across the open yards for him to come home for supper. And it was a sign to him to sin no more! To make this the last time . . . *Phyllis, I'm not going to be able to keep doing this because it's tearing me apart inside and blah blah blah.*

By dusk I was in her living room. She was making drinks for us just like in an old movie. I hadn't had a drop of hard liquor since a fraternity reunion in the early 1980s, but I agreed to scotch and water. "You've got a fireplace," I remarked as joyfully as a man who has awakened to find it was only a bad dream. From the kitchen she told me to start a fire. "There's wood in the front closet," she called to me. But all I found there were maybe fifty orange artificial logs.

All through the small talk I kept trying to picture myself back at Colgate, standing in front of the classroom and talking away with the ease and self-confidence that I took for granted before I was fired.

I'll confess to this much — the scotch went down easily and in a short time it felt like the most natural thing to do in the world was tell her about all the things that had happened since I last saw her. I don't think I was trying to win her sympathy as much as I was trying to persuade her that any idea she or I might have once had about this rendezvous turning into a romantic encounter was gone because I considered myself about as sexually undesirable as a soprano in the Vienna Boys Choir. I guess two hours passed. She kept smiling reassuringly while I talked and stole quick glances at her and then stared down at the little yacht club pennants that were painted around the rim of my cocktail glass. The only thing she responded to directly was my description of the insurance fraud, which, I think, offended her. "You shouldn't have done that," she said flatly. "If you were to die, they could deny payment to your wife. That's totally unreal," she said.

Unreal, I said to myself. That's exactly what *this* feels like.

When I shut up about myself she talked disparagingly about the guys she'd dated since college, men who expected to be waited on hand and foot. She was wearing fishnet black stockings similar to the ones I'd bought Colleen. Each time she walked into the kitchen for more scotch, her thighs made a scratching sound. I found it incredibly mesmerizing when she knocked off her high-heeled shoes and let them lay beside her feet on the floor.

"What did you have in mind for an automobile?" she finally asked.

I told her. "I don't need a brand-new one either," I said.

"Anything with fewer than seventy thousand miles would be perfect for us."

"Really, though," she said, "even with the third seat in back you're going to be cramped with four kids, a dog, and your wife."

At one point, when I came back to the living room from the bathroom, she was smiling at me with a very wise expression, as if she had figured out something about me that I didn't yet know.

"Have you read *Death of a Salesman* lately?" she wanted to know.

"No," I said honestly. I had taught Miller's play twelve times in my eight semesters at Colgate. Every student planning on majoring in English was required to take the course entitled Early American Literature. The material was astonishingly boring and bad and sent all but the most incorruptible academic geeks into deep slumber, and until I came to town with a new bag of tricks, the course was universally hated and maligned by students. I took *Death of a Salesman* and sewed it into all the old texts, tracing the modern collapse of the American Dream through the pre-American ideas about the American Dream. The class became so popular that word spread all the way to the science department, where most of the premed students began fulfilling their single humanities requirement in English by taking my course. Of course I was so flattered that I expanded the class size from twenty to thirty, and after I was notifed of my firing I pretty much canned the old texts completely and devoted almost the whole semester to the Loman family.

I confided to her that lately I hadn't been able to face Willy Loman. "It's a little too close now, you know?"

She knew, and her expression changed to one of pure sympathy. "But I think of you as Biff," she told me as she held out a fresh glass of scotch.

Oh Christ, I thought.

"The golden boy who gets lost?" she said.

"Why does he get lost?" I asked her.

"Because he believed all the silly sentimental ideas that Willy held out there for him."

I took a big gulp of booze while she smiled and said, "That was my grandfather too. He saved all his money, and rather than put my father through college he gave it all to the church. He was foolish, just like Willy. I always think of that scene where Willy has just been fired and he goes to Charley, his only real friend, to borrow money, and he just can't understand how Howard could have fired him. You remember what he says?"

I answered right away. "He says, 'How could Howard fire me? I named him when he was an infant.' "

She laughed. "Yes. And Charley says — I know it verbatim — Charley says, 'When are you gonna realize that those things don't mean anything? You named him, but you can't *sell* that. The only thing you got in this world is what you can sell. And the funny thing is that you're a salesman, and you don't know that.'

"It's beautiful, isn't it? My grandfather wanted to be liked and he wanted to believe that sentimental things like friendship and loyalty counted."

I interrupted and said, rather weakly, that things like friendship and loyalty should be more than just sentimental.

"Sure," she said, dismissing me. "And Willy desperately wanted to be liked. Remember? He thought that if he was liked, he would end up fine. He wouldn't go broke or lose the respect of his sons."

Suddenly she seemed much smarter than I remembered her. I began to sense that she was zeroing in on something.

"Willy starts to tell Charley that he always thought that if a

113

man was impressive and well liked, that nothing bad would happen to him. And Charley says — I know this whole part too; you remember, you put it on our final exam? He says to Willy, 'Why must everybody *like* you? Who liked J. P. Morgan? Was he impressive? In a Turkish bath he'd look like a butcher. But with his pockets on he was very well liked.'

"I love that line, *with his pockets on.*"

She put me in her spare bedroom. I counted five pleated tennis skirts in her closet and then slept like a dead man. The next morning she drove a Ford Bronco very fast right through the downtown while pointing out to me the different buildings and businesses her father had owned and sold over the years when she was growing up. She had that light in her eyes that used to wake me up in my eight-thirty literature class, and I leaned back in the seat and just let her drive. She showed me where she had gone to high school, the courts where she had played tennis and where Arthur Ashe had once hit balls around with her. "He was a friend of my coach," she said. I pictured her in one of those magnificent tennis skirts.

We passed the cemetery where her grandfather was buried and she slowed the car down and began telling me about how he had come to America from Italy and worked as a tile maker. I was thinking about the young men who sold cars for her, how they must fall asleep at night dreaming of marrying her.

I kept waiting for the city to flatten out and for the low-slung car dealerships and the strip malls to appear ahead of us. Instead we parked in a small lot behind a tall brick building and took the elevator to a suite of glass and chrome offices.

"You don't work at the car place?" I asked stupidly.

"My office is here," she said. "I go there a couple times a week, though."

A homely girl with an acne-scarred face brought us cinnamon-flavored coffee in glass mugs and hot cross buns that tasted so good I planned to eat the four left on the plate the minute no one was looking.

When she told me at the airport that she had had a terrific crush on me it was clear to me that she was describing someone who belonged to her distant past. "To tell you the truth," she said, "after four years of prep school and then Colgate I got a little sick of golden boys like Biff Loman. My father calls them fakers. You know, these boys who think they're entitled to some sort of special life and that they won't have to go to work every day at some kind of regular job to pay their way like the rest of us. I've fired a few golden boys since I've been here."

It hit me like a rock and I was trying to catch my breath, I think, when she said that she really did want to help me get a car. "You're sure you want the station wagon?" she asked. "The monthly payments are pretty steep."

"I thought the car might be free," I said sarcastically and wondered how in God's name I had actually believed thirty-six hours earlier that this might be in the cards.

She smiled again, and said she knew that I was too proud to accept charity. "Just like Willy," she said.

We left it that in exchange for the credit line and the car I would help write her essays for the MBA programs she was applying to. All she asked was a first draft and outline. She gave me a paperback book, called *The Princeton Review,* on the nation's top business schools. It included sample essays that promised to tell you how to perfect your application. On the cover there was a photograph of an attaché case, a laptop computer, and the *Wall Street Journal.*

I couldn't face going home. In the airport I rented a car and drove up to Bangor to see how Bradford was doing. It was raining, and the city appeared as I remembered it from my boyhood, like an old woman who tries hard but can no longer get her lipstick on straight, and there is always a loose strap sliding off her shoulder, and at parties when she sits down she forgets to close her knees.

The towering maple trees on West Broadway were tossing in the wind and the cars were stopping for people to take pictures of Stephen King's house. Bradford lived next door. It was his tennis night. We played at an indoor place. I spent most of the match watching him to see if the MS had affected his game. We were sitting in his car in his driveway when I told him that I was probably not going to come up with a teaching job for the fall and that this meant it would be another whole year before I could work again.

"What do you mean?" he asked.

"No openings until the next school year," I said.

"Yeah, but you'll be broke long before that. You'll have to find something." He told me I would have to take any job I could find and tough it out until something better came along. "Colleen's going to have to find a job too," he said. He said it so flatly that it pissed me off.

"Look," I said, "you wouldn't work for five bucks an hour."

"I would if that was the best I could do," he told me.

I let this pass. He ripped open a bag of Cheese Doodles and for a little while we were sixteen again in this city, sitting in his father's car, eating whatever we'd snuck from his mother's pantry. I reminded him how I used to move into his house whenever his parents went out of town and the maid was left in charge. I'd show up the instant his folks drove out of the driveway. One time they forgot something and came back a few minutes after I arrived and John hid me in the closet off his bedroom. It was built into the slanting roof line and I was too tall to stand up. I was bent over a pretzel can waiting for his parents to drive off again. Hours went by. Finally I risked coming out. Downstairs I found Bradford asleep on his parents' big bed.

He laughed so hard that he blew a mouthful of Cheese Doodles across the dashboard of his car.

"What's so funny?" I said. "I'm still trying to get what you've had all your life."

Soon we were sitting there in his car and I was yelling at him. A hundred yards from where we were parked was the path we had taken to school every day in seventh grade. And the little mom-and-pop store where we'd spent our hot lunch money on cream-filled pastries and soft drinks. I was aware of that. And just down the hill was the old movie theater where we'd watched *The Graduate* and *Doctor Zhivago* and felt ourselves actually changed in some way when the lights came back on. Look at us, I thought— we're sitting here in our tennis clothes, in a BMW, our faces illuminated by the lights of the car telephone. "We're disqualified from talking about the poor," I said.

"How about talking about *you,* then," he said softly after a few minutes of silence. "About you not facing reality."

"That's not what this is about," I told him.

"It's not? It seems to me that's exactly what this is about. You may have to work two or three shitty jobs next year to pay your bills. Hell, you may have to live in a mobile home—plenty of decent people do. You've been expecting great big things to happen to you for as long as I can remember. For Colleen's sake, and for the kids', you're going to have to grow up."

117

9

IRS $3,000. Ohio trip $675.00. Car rental for Bangor trip $59.00. Electricity $112.45. Life insurance $338.00. Food? Miscellaneous $88.00.

B A L A N C E *July 15: $7,141.79*

I don't offer this as an excuse, but I think that the reason I ran around like a man chasing his hat in a gale for the rest of that summer is because I was still under the influence of the great false belief of my generation that life is more about fate than accommodation.

I thought I would knock off the graduate school essays in one morning's work lying in bed and win us a Ford station wagon, but all the questions on the applications concerned the *future* of American capitalism, and since the future of everything looked so bleak to me I kept writing one somber paragraph after another that amounted to a lugubrious lament for the passing of culture and civilization. I wasn't able to shake the thought that the future, not only of business in America but of society in general, was being written in the poverty and the humiliation and the rage of the inner cities while the rest of us proceeded along blindly in our comfortable lives, bolting our doors at night and numbing ourselves with rented movies. After four days I emerged bleary-eyed from my solitude, gave up, and sent the applications back to Ohio. Then I called Dave, the mechanic, and asked him to fix the station wagon. "I know it may not be worth it," I said to him.

"Hey," he replied, "this is the only car you've got and the only car you can afford, right? So it's worth it."

Then I tried to get involved in Colleen's garden. "It's much too late," she said to me when I showed her the wooden poles I'd cut for the beans.

"But you asked me for poles?"

"That was a month ago."

I stood on the outside of the fence she had put up without my help and held out a little packet of peas I'd picked up at the Shop & Save.

"I already planted peas," she said.

"Well, we can use more, can't we?" I was looking for a way back into my family. I lay in the grass and soon Jack and Nell each found a stick for make-believe paddles and they sat on me and turned me into their canoe while I watched Colleen working in the garden. She was barefoot in the dirt. Her jeans were rolled up over her calves. I was thinking how strong she looked when suddenly she stopped working, stood up straight, leaned against the shovel handle, and bowed her head. It took me by surprise. I watched as she gently swayed against the shovel as if she were doing a slow dance with it. The kids just kept on doing what they were doing, they didn't see it or it might have surprised them too, their mother resting in the middle of the day, their mother who is remembered fondly in every neighborhood where she lived as a girl and then a woman as the person who gathered into her orbit all the other kids from around town who were driving their own parents crazy and organized them into a neighborhood parade.

Often at the end of a day she would come into the bathroom and I'd hear her say happily, "I've had to pee since before lunch, but this is the first time I've sat down all day." She took after her own mother who, as a teenaged girl, set the record for the number of barrels of potatoes picked in a single day in Presque Isle, Maine.

She's just tired, I told myself. She was tired because I was wearing her out. I had married a girl with remarkable energy and hope and optimism, a sensible girl with a beautiful simplicity of heart and an extraordinary light about her that everyone who ever met her took notice of and remembered. As I watched her in her garden, I acknowledged that all of this was being depleted. It was as if a shadow had begun to sweep across her the moment she discovered that maybe she was married to a man who could not be counted upon when the going got a little rough. She had never complained about this; it wasn't in her nature to complain. One of the reasons she always had so much energy, I think, is because she never wasted energy on things she could do nothing about.

This moment I will never forget: as Colleen leaned against the shovel and I watched her and fell into another one of my pathetic excursions into self-analysis, I looked down and saw that I had begun to drum my fingers against my thigh. Right hand, exactly the way my grandfather had done in the beginning stages of the nervous condition called Saint Vitus's dance that claimed him in his early forties. I knew this detail about him so well because I was a small boy, age four, just the right height to put me at eye level with his drumming fingers. I'd never put two and two together before, but it was clear to me now; when my mother died ten days after giving birth to me and my twin brother, my father had moved back home so my grandmother could care for us. Suddenly my grandfather, an intensely private man who had barely survived the storm of raising four children of his own, selling apples in the street during the Depression, now was faced with two more babies. I've been told that very soon after my father moved back into his father's house with us in his arms, my grandfather, a printer by trade, moved a linotype press into the back room of his small house, and that was where he took up residence, standing beside this pounding freight train of a machine that shook the house and drowned out all the baby noise beneath its thunder.

I was now roughly the same age he had been when I was dumped into his lap, and as I watched Colleen leaning against the shovel, and glanced down at my hand, I knew for certain that she was pregnant. *Oh God,* I thought, *what could be worse right now than to have a fifth baby?* As the businessman at the Little League field had said to me, a man without prospects cannot afford to relax for one minute. And a father who cannot relax passes along each anxious tremor, each nervous tick, to his newborn child.

I watched Colleen in her garden and wondered what it would be like to have an unwanted baby. Babies were all that Colleen had ever wanted. When I first began asking her how many babies she wanted, she only said, "A lot of them." This, she knew, was her life's calling, being a mother, loving and teaching her children. And it had always been so easy, so utterly effortless for her to become pregnant and to bring each baby along into childhood. I never could understand why people had so much difficulty conceiving. I was blind to their frustration and their pain. We had never practiced any kind of birth control except the old Catholic rhythm method during the three years we dated, but Colleen's internal systems and clocks were so regular that you could bet money on them. Then when we got married she decided when each baby should be conceived. She decided and kept it a secret until the third or fourth month of pregnancy. I was thirty-four years old, and, until I met her, I figured I was beyond having children. When we were in Paris, two days after we eloped in England, she decided that it was the right time to conceive our first child. She never asked me about it or told me anything. When we made love four times our first day in the city, I accepted it the way a dog would accept four bowls of food set down on the floor for its supper. And two weeks after leaving Paris, when Colleen began to fall asleep the instant her head hit the pillow and to sleep through till the next morning, I didn't have a clue that this meant anything.

In one of the apartments I lived in as a boy after my father remarried, a place where you could hear the rats running around the attic at night, there was an ancient oil furnace in the basement. It was an enormous machine made of lead and iron, with pipes and gauges, valves and levers, and rusted sheet metal tubes that reached from its heart like the tentacles of an octopus. All through the winter it would shut down without warning and our whole family would go down to the basement, my father leading the way with a flashlight, and we'd just stare at it, not knowing what to do. To stand before it was to stand dumbfounded in the presence of a fathomless mechanical mystery that only our landlord could figure out. She would arrive like Mary Poppins in a great gust of wind, march past us, rolling up her sleeves, and then disappear into the web of rusted iron and blackened sheet metal, and when she came back out, the damned thing was running again. This was how I came to regard Colleen in our world of babies. She knew from the start exactly how to interpret each of their desires, how to cure their little illnesses, how to bring them comfort. One of Colleen's doctors told me that she had high-powered breast milk, enough of it to feed quintuplets. It ran from her nipples all day long, soaking her shirts, and it contained some special quality that made our babies sleep like teenagers from their first day home from the hospital.

Colleen had presented me with contented and gorgeous red-cheeked babies whom I fell hopelessly in love with so that from the moment she first placed them in my arms I could never really get a clear picture again of what life had been like before them.

In those five years of four babies, my attitude had been, Let ordinary men plan each baby carefully, assessing what each new child would mean in terms of money and time. Bring them on! As many babies as we can have!

Now, at the prospect of another one, I caught myself drumming my fingers nervously against my thigh and thinking that everyone who knew me was going to look at me and say, For Christ's sake, what are you doing having another baby!

I fell asleep lying in the yard, watching her. When I awoke I was alone and a little disoriented. I walked around the side of the barn and saw that the kids had set up a lemonade stand in the front lawn, next to the sidewalk. I watched for a while as people stopped. Then I walked off into the woods to gather some sticks for the woodstove. I was walking around, not thinking about anything really when I turned back and realized I had gone quite far and I couldn't see the house. A strange fear came like a sudden turn in the wind. I told myself it was silly, but I began listening closely to the sounds and gradually a vision swept over me of a single man in a beat-up station wagon inviting my children for a ride. He just stops for lemonade this first time, stalking them: *"Will you be here next Saturday too? Out front here like this, right next to the road, by yourselves?"* I dropped the firewood and started running through the woods, searching for a stick I could use as a club.

At the far edge of the lawn I stopped myself when they came into view. What I might have said to them, and the look on my face, the look of a father who has lost the belief in his power to protect his children from misfortune, would have emptied their hearts. So I sat in the scrub pines and watched them secretly.

The next morning I walked to the gas station in Falmouth, paid Dave for the car, and then drove straight into Portland and made my way to the state employment office on Prebble Street. It was a flat-roofed, windowless one-story brick building that looked like a minimum security prison. Outside the front doors men and women in Salvation Army clothes smoked and stared down at the sidewalk. There was an El Camino parked at the corner a few feet away. Its top was down and a woman with frosted hair had one bare foot up on the dashboard and was painting her toenails lavender.

Inside I got in line behind a Vietnamese man and a big-shouldered hooligan who was shouting at the woman behind the counter — "But I told you, I can do that job! I got tools!"

The woman kept apologizing and he kept shouting. The Vietnamese man turned to me and said sorrowfully, "No address, no work."

The women who worked the counter were pleasant and firm, like nurses. They were trained to call our names out loud, first and last, when it was our turn, but you could see on their faces that they didn't want to do this, they didn't relish making our failure a public matter. They handed us forms to fill out and a brochure published by the city of Portland with forty-seven helpful hints for the unemployed. *Look for coupons in the newspapers . . . Disconnect your cable television.*

"I have an address," I told the woman when it was my turn, "but no tools."

She raised her eyebrows and said, "An address is a good start. Do you have reliable transportation?"

"I do."

"And what kind of work are you looking for?"

"Anything," I said, "as long as it carries health insurance. I think my wife is going to have a baby."

She stopped writing and looked up at me. When she explained that even if I found work that offered insurance there would be a waiting period that would exclude this pregnancy, I pretended to know this. My God, I thought, I've been protected for so long that I don't have any idea how the world works anymore.

I began returning to the office at the same time every morning to ask the same woman for the same thing each time— "Work with health insurance for my family, please"— and from the first day I believed that somebody would pick me out of the crowd waiting in lines there and lead me to a desk where the really sweet jobs were handed out to the special people with graduate degrees and a certain refinement. I confided to the woman that I was having nightmares about the kids getting sick. The cheapest insurance policy for a family of six was over six hundred dollars a month, and all I wanted was some kind of work that would place us among the insured.

Each day she checked her computer printouts and shook her head. "Nothing yet. I'm sorry."

The expressions on the faces of those who waited with me broke down cleanly into two categories. Proud shock— *I never expected to be here* . . . Or resignation— *What do you expect from a bum like me?* The tiny Vietnamese men were always there, and even though the kind ladies had trouble with their names, the men always smiled and did a kind of half bow from the waist when they were called. They kept smiling and bowing as if to compensate for the burden they had become. I recalled the beggars in England, waiting in line outside the London theaters for free seats given to the *unwaged*. Nourishment for the soul. How nice, I thought, if one of the ladies would lead all of us here up the sidewalk, down Elm Street like a second grade class on a field trip from school, up Congress Street to Portland's Symphony Hall to hear Mahler's Third.

For a few days I brought along Saul Bellow's novel *Herzog* so I could feel a little better than everyone else waiting in line. A little careless. But while I waited in line I wrote out my budgets inside the front and back covers. Standing there, I wrote the next year away, wrote it right out of existence, feeling some degree of safety accounting for things this way. The executive pencils in a lunch date two months away, and he believes nothing can happen to him in the intervening sixty days. Our budget would protect us from whatever vagaries haunt the unemployed and the poor. In the crowded unemployment office, under the fluorescent tubes, I tried to disappear into the numbers. Food for the rest of the summer *$400*. Dentist *$250*. Telephone *$50*. Car insurance *$240*. Electricity *$80*. Car repairs *$1,378*. By the end of summer, $4,700 left. My goal was to find work before we got below $4,000, to keep that little cushion.

One day at the employment office I left the line at the counter to use the men's room. When I opened the door there was this tiny Vietnamese man standing at the sink. He was running hot water over a Tupperware container that was filled with horrible-looking congealed gravy with chunks of meat sticking in it. It made me feel like throwing up. But the little man turned and smiled at me and gave me a little bow and said, "Better hot. Very good hot." It hit me how hard some people work just to live in this country and how their spirit rises indomitably above the meagerness of their circumstances. Why couldn't I be that way for Colleen and my children? Why had I turned out to be a man who could only be happy when things were going well?

I didn't know why until the letter came from Princeton telling me that I was not on the short list of candidates they were inviting to campus to interview for the job. At the moment I read the letter I knew why I couldn't walk the streets of Portland looking for a job waiting tables in a restaurant for tips, or working in a bookstore. It's simple, really; when you have been spoiled — and by this I mean when you have had *the chance* to work hard in a meaningful profession that affords you comfort and stimulation, a chance denied those in the ghetto and many of those in my generation who went to fight in Vietnam — there is the irresistible impulse to let fate run its course. I wanted us to live to the end of our money and our security in order to find out whether I would be rescued by fate, and if not, whether I would find the courage to meet the price.

One night after the kids were asleep Colleen called me into the bathroom, where she was lying in the tub. "Baths are great," she said with a sigh when I came in. "My second favorite thing."

"I'll wash your back for you," I said. I knelt down beside the tub.

She said, "I know there isn't any such thing as heaven, but if there was and they didn't have taking baths and making love there, then heaven wouldn't compare to life here. Not for me, anyway."

I held her hair up with one hand and washed her back with the other.

Out of the blue she told me that she had been thinking about a woman we once knew who had been unable to bring a baby to full term. "When Ellen O'Connor had all those miscarriages, I told her brother once that I'd love to have a baby for her. I thought that we could live near them so I could watch the baby from a distance. I've always thought it was one of the best things a woman could do, and you know how I love being pregnant, that part is easy. But I wouldn't want them all in the delivery room the way that some people do it. And really, I don't think I'd want to know the mother. If she has bad taste or something dumb like that, it would bother me. I know that's stupid, but to always picture the baby growing up in a house with plastic curtains on the windows . . ."

I expected her to tell me next why she was thinking about this, but she didn't and I didn't ask her.

"The people who want babies," she said. "Have you ever read their advertisements in the newspaper? Can you imagine how desperate they must be. I feel so sorry for them."

"You're the last person on earth who could give up a baby," I told her. I waited for her to deny this.

"Do you think the time is coming when we won't be able to keep our children safe in this country?" she asked.

I told her not to worry.

"But I do," she said. "I don't worry about the short-term things, I know we'll get by somehow. But sometimes I think about the future, our grandchildrens' future, and their children. It frightens me."

She had never spoken this way before and I leaned over the tub and laid my cheek on her back to try to reassure her. "What about us?" she asked. "Is something happening to you and me? Because if there is, I'm going to be really pissed off at you, Don J. Snyder. And if you ever leave us, you'll be making a big mistake."

"What are you talking about?" I said.

She looked at me and shook her head.

"Everything's going to be okay," I said.

She wasn't listening. "And don't start thinking the way some men do, that everything will be better if you find someone else."

"I won't," I said.

"Good. Because if you do, we won't be friends — you won't come by and visit us and buy nice things for the kids. I'll take them and we'll move far away and start a new life without you. That's the only way I could stand it."

I looked into her eyes. "Okay," I said.

A few days later the father of one of my favorite students wrote to me out of the blue with word that his son had suffered a nervous breakdown. In his letter he said he wanted to meet with me as soon as possible to talk about the boy and he enclosed his telephone number and asked me to call him collect. I had never met the man but I knew that he had made a small fortune in computer software and that his son, during the three years I knew him, wished to become a poet.

That night Colleen was dressing the kids in our bedroom when I came upstairs with the letter for her to read. She looked up at me when I came in. "I love summer nights the best," she said. "Don't the kids look so beautiful after their baths on nights like this?"

For her, the measure of the world's beauty was in the children who inhabit it, and what was astonishing to me was that she took the time to observe this beauty even when her world was tilting off its center. She hadn't said anything to me about being pregnant and, except for our conversation about having a baby for a woman who was unable to conceive, and the way she leaned against her shovel in the garden, all I had was an intuition. But it was strong and I had started leaving the daily newspapers on the kitchen table, opened to the classified section where childless couples cast their lines upon the water under the heading *Adoption*. They filled their small space with words that promoted their worthiness. *Christian couple with large home and garden. Active, loving, financially secure couple. Couple lives and works on country club grounds. Christian professional couple. Stable married couple.* These people understood the economics surrounding unwanted babies, the financial details that were implicit in an exchange. In each ad you could hear the same promise: "*I have the money to pay for food, clothing, braces, medical attention, college.*"

Each time I read these notices in the newspaper I wondered how much money the childless couples paid for babies, and now as Colleen cradled Cara in her arms and read the letter from my student's father I began to think that fate was intervening. Just as I was considering asking Colleen to give up this baby whose existence had not yet been articulated, this wealthy father was appealing to me for help. The iron wheel was rolling along the track.

When I called him later that night and listened to his anxious voice on the telephone, I pictured him standing inside a beautiful house somewhere in one of those wooded suburbs outside Boston. Maybe he rode in a hunt club on fall weekends. There was a desk somewhere in his house where he had sat to write out all those tuition checks for Colgate. Maybe he would write one for us, and maybe he would be so grateful to me that he would give me a job in his company. "*I'll be glad to go speak to your son, but of course I'll have to ask you for something up front. I mean—*"

"*No, no. No need to explain . . . Is five thousand satisfactory?*"

"*Well, yes. As a matter of fact, that will cover the hospital cost for the new baby.*"

He asked me if I had time to meet with him the next day. "I'm an hour north of Boston," he said.

"I can meet you tomorrow," I told him.

"What time?"

"I'm pretty much free all day tomorrow," I said. *And the next day, and the day after that,* I thought.

As it turned out, Billy's father was a modest little Irishman with a few strands of dark hair drawn carefully across his head. He had brought a picture of Billy. Actually it was a family photograph, a staged affair with mother, father, and four children all dressed up in front of a Christmas tree. The Billy I had known carried his skateboard everywhere he went on campus and wore exotically mismatched rags that resembled conventional clothing only in the number of openings they had for arms and legs.

I'd known him to be a reasonably happy kid who kept busy on weekends taking long excursions on his mountain bike or cross-country skis. The face in this photograph bore the tense expression of a hostage trying to communicate to his audience that he was being held captive against his will.

In the first hour his father told me three or four times how much it would mean to Billy's mother if I were to take the time to go see him. She had been the one to go through his bedroom closet after he became sick and to find the letter he'd written me but never mailed, and by the way the father spoke of her I got the impression that she was pretty close to some kind of breakdown herself.

"He's our firstborn," the father said. "His mother blames herself even though I was the one who pushed him to take a summer job with one of the banks in town. He didn't seem to mind, other than complaining about the dress code. He called his jacket and tie his monkey suit."

He smiled briefly when he recounted this, and then the smile vanished and he got a far-off look in his eyes. "He worked there six weeks and then he just quit. He just laid on the couch on a Friday morning and never got up again except to go to the bathroom. Doctors don't use the term *nervous breakdown* anymore, but a good friend of mine, the one who got Billy into the clinic at Yale, told me his condition met all the criteria for exactly that."

We were walking together along a beautiful stretch of beach and he seemed like he wanted to talk forever. I had the impression that he was one of those men who had pretty much kept silent his whole life until this trouble came along. He told me about his own childhood, the blue-collar neighborhood in Belmont, Massachusetts, where everyone had seemed fairly happy. Fathers worked hard, but they were able to afford to buy a home and many of them eventually put their kids through college. "It's all changed," he said sadly. "I'm not blaming your generation — hell, I'm not that much older than you are. But what's missing is the way people used to help each other. There was a kind of unofficial apprenticeship that young men went through. You know, the guys in their late thirties would take the time to point the way for the younger fellows. It was nothing new, it had been that way since medieval days, but it seemed to vanish with your generation. Every guy was just looking out for himself, and life got much harder for young people. I see that everyday in the business world where I work. And maybe I wanted Billy just to land a job and not try to do something different and extraordinary with himself. I know he started writing poetry in your class, and even though I couldn't understand most of it, I thought it was pretty good. But I guess I never thought he was tough enough for that kind of life."

I rode another bus, this one with movies. No one was talking or looking out the windows. We all had our heads back on the white paper doilies, staring straight ahead, all of us completely absorbed by the images on the screen. For a minute I thought about the day my father carried our first television set into our house. It was 1956 and all along the street the other fathers were doing the same thing. Ours was enshrined in such a huge and heavy wood cabinet that Tommy Moyers's dad had to help my father get it into the living room. And what splendor, that box of light and sound. So improbable and so beautiful. All the houses on my street were identical and the living room furniture in every house had always been arranged to face the fireplace until the televisions arrived and everything was turned in their direction.

In Boston I boarded a train and thought about Billy for most of the trip. I remembered how he had persuaded the campus food service at the university to give him leftover food after lunch for a homeless shelter in Syracuse. He had been disappointed that the food was stone cold by the time he got it to the shelter, and so he went about finding a takeout restaurant to donate ten thousand Styrofoam trays with lids.

The nearer I got to Billy the more certain I was that what had been unspoken between his father and me was my contribution to his son's discontent. I had been the professor who encouraged him to write poetry. He had come to me at the end of his freshman year asking me for a list of books to read over the summer. I thought of those books as the train rolled on toward Connecticut. The writing of Rilke, Dickinson, Steinbeck, Whitman. All of it depressing as hell and bound to drive a wedge between his world and his father's world of software. I saw this so clearly en route to New Haven that the picture I'd originally painted in my mind — there I am presenting a rehabilitated Billy to his grateful parents, a completely restored Billy who once again believes all the things one must believe in order to get up off the living room couch — was pathetic to me.

I wasn't prepared for how pale and thin he looked. He was dressed in jeans with both knees ripped out and a stained white dress shirt I thought he might have worn to his job at the bank. I shook his hand and tried to make him laugh by recounting what had happened to me just as the train pulled in. I had been standing in the place between two cars, right behind a beautiful woman who was as close to the door as she could get. We were both waiting for the door to open, so I said hello. She turned and looked at me with the kind of expression you'd save for meeting a serial killer. Then the door opened and this great blast of wind threw her dress right up over her head so that suddenly she was standing right next to me in only her bra and panties. "I saw everything," I told him. "She looked like a tulip. I almost reached out and helped pull her dress back down."

Billy laughed, but you could tell that his heart wasn't in it. "We're vulnerable when we least expect it, aren't we?" he said.

We walked to the parking lot where he had left his beat-up car. He asked me if I would drive him to the drugstore so he could refill his prescriptions.

The pharmacist greeted him by name and set all five containers of pills on the counter, looking at me with a concerned expression. She took the time to go over all the instructions while Billy struggled to read the small print with a pair of cheap gold-framed costume jewelry magnifying glasses he told me he had bought in the hospital gift shop when his medication made him lose his vision.

The instructions were so confusing that I knew I wouldn't be able to help him later on if he hadn't understood the pharmacist, so I asked for one of those little containers old people use to help them keep their daily doses straight.

Billy used his arm and swept all the bottles into his pocket. "Here's your change," the pharmacist called to him, but he walked away, explaining to me that he hadn't been able to carry change in his pockets all summer because it reminded him of how his father used to jingle his change as an expression of his authority.

I joked with him about his glasses. "Get a cardigan sweater and one of those little chains to hang your glasses around your neck and you might get a job as a librarian."

"I always had perfect vision," he said somberly.

In his apartment the only thing hanging on the walls was an aerial photograph of a lake in the woods. "Do you recognize the place?" he asked me, and when I didn't he said it was Walden Pond.

"What part of the pond did Hank build his cabin on?"

"Hank?"

"Henry D."

I didn't know.

"I loved that book," he said. "The way you described his life to us, it made perfect sense."

I looked across the room at him. He was leaning against the front door as if he were expecting an enemy to attack.

"Look," I said, "I really never knew that much about Thoreau's work. I never even read *Walden Pond* when I was in college."

I waited for him to react to this, but he glided right across it. "My favorite, though, was *Grapes of Wrath*. It stirred me, you know. Man, if you read that book and still believe that business and capitalism don't rip the bones right out of people, then you'd better read it again."

He looked over at me suddenly as if he had just remembered that I was there in the room with him.

"If you can stay awhile, you can sleep in my bed. I love the couch."

"I love sleeping on couches," I told him.

"Okay, then you take the couch," he said.

He checked his watch and told me that in ten minutes he was going to have to turn on the television.

"I know you hate TV," he said.

"Why do you say that?"

"You always knocked television in class."

I felt this little bubble of panic rising into the back of my throat. "Listen, Billy," I said, "you have to forget everything I ever said when I was your professor."

He ignored this and turned the television to one of the afternoon talk shows. "I watch these all the time," he told me with a smile. The panelists that day were middle-aged women who had been reunited with the boys who took their virginity. During one commercial he told me about his routine in the mental ward. "They would read the newspaper to us first thing each morning, and then we'd play Trivial Pursuit. My first question on the little card was, 'Which is the more tender in a chicken, the right breast

136

or the left breast?' I don't know why I said it, but I said left breast, and I was right."

The temperature got up into the nineties and the only fan that Billy had was one he'd found at a yard sale for fifty cents. It had lost all but the highest speed, and when it was on it roared like an airplane propeller and scattered the newspaper around the living room. We worked out an arrangement where we talked for ten-minute intervals, then ran the fan for ten minutes to clear the airless room. He seemed oblivious to the roar even when I shouted above it that we should try to play some tennis. He merely nodded and we began a process of trying to find his racket and sneakers. It took nearly half an hour, and we were both soaked in sweat when we were ready to go out the door into the hot sun. We walked to a park and as soon as the tennis courts came into view he told me he was too tired to play.

While he slept I went around looking at his things. An expensive-looking telescope in pieces on the floor. Four sand dollars in a small box like the kind banks use to send out new checks. The only books he had on his shelf were ones I had assigned in my literature courses that he had taken at Colgate. I opened his copy of *Grapes of Wrath* and the photograph of Patty Hearst dressed in combat fatigues and brandishing a machine gun fell to the floor.

That night after we took a walk through town he asked me if I would read to him from *Walden Pond*. He put his head back and shut his eyes and I read to him just like I would have been reading to my kids if I had been at home. And like them, he fell asleep, though it was early. I went outside for a while and I heard drums off in the distance. Not the kind of drumming in a band, but the slow rolling of drums, like the kind in funeral marches. It sent a chill through me. I didn't want to spend even one night in his stifling apartment. I kept thinking how easy it would be for me to pack all his belongings in his car and start driving him home to Maine to live with us. I fell asleep that night with my head at the propeller of the big fan.

At sunrise the next morning the drummers were gathering on the green in the center of town for a second day of mustering. I bought a newspaper in Cumberland Farms and stood in line next to one of the soldiers, a little man in a hurry to bring back a case of Coke to his fellow comrades in arms. He had pale, yellow skin, so pale it was nearly translucent, and hair standing straight up on the top of his head and shaved above his ears. His face bore no expression. His uniform consisted of shiny black shoes, a wide, black leather belt with a hook on it for the drum, another for the pewter mug, and two slots for the drumsticks. The high-tech glasses he was wearing made the outfit seem utterly unconvincing. I watched him for a long time as he walked back to the green, and I wondered if people who have nervous breakdowns end up like this, as small, lost souls who send away for drummer's outfits from some mail-order house so that they can belong to bands that spend weekends marching in formation in town squares and village greens along the Connecticut coastline.

For a while I watched Billy sleeping faceup on the couch, his hands occasionally reaching in his medicated dream as if he were trying to swim to the ceiling.

"Mustard?" he said when I woke him. "I'm sorry, I don't understand?"

"No. A *muster* on the green in town," I said.

Later we managed a walk to the soccer field, where some middle-aged Spanish-speaking men played a lazy game of soccer. Out of the blue, Billy told me that the most frightening part of being in the hospital was when patients were forced to leave because their allotted insurance payment or subsidy ran out. One woman had to be carried out, screaming, "I can't go grocery shopping! I'll get lost!"

"That place changed me," he said.

The whole time he talked about his breakdown, he kept raking his hair back with his right hand, raking it harder and harder and stopping to examine his fingernails from time to time as if to see if he was drawing blood. He told me that he had taken the bank job for the summer to please his parents, but then he began to like it. There were a bunch of cool people working there and they started doing things together on the weekends.

I was waiting for him to tell me more, maybe to say that he'd met some nice young women, but he just stopped there and gazed vacantly at the soccer game.

It took a violent thunderstorm finally to quiet the rattling drums at midnight. Before he fell asleep, Billy told me that his parents were thinking about getting a divorce. He blamed himself for this, claiming that they hadn't had any troubles until he moved home for the summer.

"It sucked," he said sadly. "I felt like the guy in that story by Kafka, the guy who turns into a bug and lives in his bedroom and his family ends up hating him. My mom kept bringing more food to my room. And my dad kept giving me the names of people who might hire me when I finished college if I did well in the bank. They were all contacts of his."

When I asked him how long he was at the bank job he said he didn't have any idea. I watched him slide down in the chair as he got into it, and I suddenly felt sad as hell for him. I thought about how sharp his mind had been when he was a student and how I had never prepared any of my students for the boredom that sets in after college or for the bleakness of rented apartment rooms like the one we were sitting in. I thought about the drugs washing through his brains. The pills left a thin line of white foam on his lips, and I wondered if any of my children would notice this were I to crack up like Billy.

He told me that he was surprised when things at the bank turned sour. "I'd just gone out and bought these three suits. Here, let me show you."

He went into his bedroom and took a long time. I thought about the businessman at the Little League field whose suits no longer fit him. When Billy came back into the room he was wearing one suit and carrying the other two. "I look the part, don't I?" he asked. "Or can you tell?"

"Tell what?"

"You know, tell that I'm an imposter?" He laughed hard at this with his eyes opened wide. "Look at this suit, though. It's beautiful, isn't it? I could be anything in a suit like this. My monkey suit. I was wearing it when I joined the club at the bank. Every Friday afternoon we'd sit around this dude's office and make phone calls to slackers. They were all black customers and their lives had turned to shit. We'd hook up for a conference call and just berate these people. *Hey, nigger, I hope you got a good heater in your Cadillac because that's where you're going to be spending the winter!* That kind of stuff. We all did it. It was like a big football game or something. Everybody was trying to come up with the best stuff. Even the girls at the bank did it. When I quit the job, it was because I felt dirty. I kept taking all these hot showers, but I still felt dirty. I quit. I just left a message on the president's desk. My dad's friend."

He said he had something to show me and he disappeared

again into the bedroom. When he returned he was carrying some good-sized rocks, baseball-sized at least, and he lined them up on top of the television.

"My trophies," he said with another hard laugh. "I don't know why, but I started breaking windows a little while ago. I dress up in my monkey suit and I go ride around the executive neighborhoods and throw rocks through windows. I've probably broken fifty or sixty. Lately I've felt like doing that. I don't know why." He bowed his head and ran his hand over the rocks on top of the television. "Boy," he said, "my folks would freak out if they knew this."

He sat down on the floor, crossed his legs and arms, and began rocking from side to side.

"Look," I said, "this seems like a lonely way to live, Billy. Why don't you come stay with us in Maine for a while. Just until . . . you know, until —"

He cut me off. "I've got this cool video of Patty Hearst robbing a bank in San Diego. I ordered it through a magazine. I'd like to fight like she did. I drive around the nice neighborhoods and I think, well, shit, this is what's out there for me. All those days I went to school and did what I was told, kept my mouth shut. This is the world that was going to be mine? And in all the houses I think about people who do the kind of shit I did when I called those black people up and screamed at them on the phone. I just want to be like Tom Joad, is all. You know what Tom said. 'I gotta keep moving, outrun them all for as long as I can.' "

He drove me to the train station the next morning. I had misread the timetable and we got there an hour early. I went into a little store and bought us each a bottle of apple juice. I thought we could sit outside in the sun and wait for my train.

"Listen," I said when we sat down on a park bench, "there aren't any Tom Joads. Tom was invented by Steinbeck, that's all."

He smiled. "That's what my mom told me. She wanted to let me off the hook just like you do. I know there are heroes out there who don't cave in."

How could I deny this? I'd wanted to be one myself and even believed for a long time that I *was* one. I can't recall what I said next. Whatever it was, he disregarded it and said he had to go.

"I feel bad about this," he said, "but I can't wait here with you. I feel like I have to get back home now."

I watched him drive away. I felt that he had just gotten tired of my company, or maybe that he was disappointed to find that I was just like all the rest of the people who were trying to push him toward a road that led back into the system he believed he would forever remain an outsider to. I left there afraid that Billy would find out that I had come to see him because I was hoping that his father would offer me something. Billy was one of the students at Colgate who had put himself on the line for me, protesting against the administration when I was fired. He had demanded a meeting with the university president and then a forum where the president was forced to explain to hundreds of students why I had been released. Someone told me the next day that the president had offered a politically correct explanation to the crowd and Billy stood up and shouted at him, "That's not good enough!"

I think it was the next day when Billy's father called to thank me. I remember as clearly as if it were yesterday that I was still thinking perhaps he would repay me for my effort. I fought back the urge to ask him if he could find a place for me in his software company. At least I managed to do that.

I wanted to do something for Billy, something meaningful,

and I decided I would go through my boxes of books and find the ones I'd assigned to him to read when he was my student, and I would find passages in those books I could send him to encourage him. But once I got started I began reading the notations I had made in the margins of the pages, notes for my classroom lectures. It was clear to me in those moments that I had never read any of this literature purely for the sake of learning; I had always been looking for something in these texts that would make me appear clever in class or before my colleagues. Lines I could drop at parties, imagining the dean's wife recalling later as she slipped into bed, "*Oh, you know, that droll, charming young man in the English department?*"

I got some trash bags from the kitchen and began going through all my books, separating the ones that I'd written in. But soon I decided to put them all in trash bags, along with more than a dozen spiral notebooks that contained the notes for my lectures.

In the morning at first light I drove to the town dump in Yarmouth. I was the first car there, waiting outside the gates when they opened. "Whatcha got there?" the toothless man in charge of the landfill asked.

"An old life," I said.

He looked at me then pointed to the trash bags piled on the front seat next to me. "Open that one," he said. I did, and when I told him all I had was books, he made me take them to where a brushfire was smoldering on top of a hill.

Instead of just dropping all the bags in the fire, I opened each bag and threw in one book at a time. There was a big pile of Sears Roebuck catalogs smoldering in the ashes and I threw my books on top of them. The complete works of Emily Dickinson and Melville. Hawthorne's *Scarlet Letter*. My beat-up hardcover copy of Miller's *Death of a Salesman*. I looked through it and read all the passages that the girl in Ohio had memorized. I came to the part where Charley, Willy's best friend, offers to save Willy by giving him a job. Willy is too proud to take it and he tells Charley, "I've got a job." Charley says, "Without pay? What kind of a job is a job without pay?" I remembered the lecture I had written around those few lines and how I always ended that class session by telling my students that this was precisely the kind of job they should pray to have one day, a job they loved so much that they would do it without pay. I'd been pleased with myself for this, but now as I read the lines I saw myself as the worst kind of phony, standing in front of students, painting a romantic picture of the life of an outsider, a life I knew nothing about.

In that day's mail there were three more job rejection letters. I read them and left them on the kitchen counter.

10

Telephone $45.25. Food $313.70. Car repairs
$1,378.00. Connecticut trip $65.44. Miscellaneous
$176.00.

BALANCE *August 2: $5,163.40*

Each time I looked at Colleen I thought she was beginning to fill out her clothes. With each pregnancy a little path of freckles had appeared across the bridge of her nose, and when I saw its faint outline one morning while she lay in bed sleeping, I called the Prosperous Christian Couple with Love and Security to Give a Child.

I used the telephone in town outside Donatelli's restaurant, and I told the whole truth and nothing but the truth except for small lies about my name and the town where I lived. The woman had such a sweet voice. "We'd love to have you and your wife for dinner guests," she said.

Dinner guests.

"Wait, Edmund is going to the upstairs phone," she said.

He picked up and said, "Hello, I'm Edmund. It's very good to talk to you. Would you and your wife come out for lunch?"

"I invited them for dinner, honey," his wife said.

He began apologizing.

"I could come for coffee," I said.

"Oh, yes," she said. "When?"

I told her that I would be there in an hour. She began giving me directions to their house, but in her eagerness she couldn't seem to find a way from the Yarmouth library, where I said I would be driving from. "Here, honey," her husband said tenderly. "Why don't you hang up now and I'll give the directions."

I didn't have anything to wear. Nothing appropriate. I stood in my boxer shorts trying things on before the tall mirror in the bedroom. Relieved that the couple had sounded so friendly on the telephone, I speculated that we would talk about money at this first meeting. Some ballpark figure maybe, so I would have a number to plug into my budgets. All Colleen had ever wanted from life was a large family and the chance to stay at home with the kids until they began school. In the ten years I had known her, she had never asked me for anything else. This dream had been in place long before I came along, and when we met she was still in college, holding down three jobs as a full-time student so that she wouldn't graduate beneath a mountain of debt that would force her to spend her youth working to pay it off instead of having babies. In the end I put on my old ripped blue jeans and decided to tell the couple that I had just been working in the garden. *I can only stay a few minutes. I have to get home and finish mowing the lawn.*

I had Cara in my arms when I walked out the kitchen door. Colleen was sitting on the porch brushing the knots out of Nell's hair. I told them that I was going to town for gas for the lawn mower. "I'll take Cara for the ride."

"That's nice," Colleen said. "Kiss us goodbye."

I leaned over and kissed them both.

"Oh, wait," Colleen said. "What do you have all over your face, sweetie? You can't go out on a date with Daddy looking like a ditchdigger."

I told her it was okay, but she went inside and came back with a wet washcloth. As she washed Cara's cheeks and brushed her hair I wondered if there was a day ahead of us, maybe a month away, or a year, or five years, when I would be able to tell Colleen how much it hurt to watch her making Cara pretty, an unwitting participant in my selfish scheme, and how I had felt something shut off inside me, something that I couldn't name. I stood there as long as I could and then I took the brush from her and ran it across the top of my head. "Do I look all right?" I asked her.

When we got to their house, I couldn't bring myself to stop. I rolled past slowly and in the rearview mirror I saw a beautiful white station wagon in the driveway. There were louvered shades on all the windows that faced the street. It was a big white house with dark green trim, three brick chimneys, geraniums in a large pot by the front door.

The next time I drove by, a few days later, I was alone, and just as I turned the corner onto their street the white station wagon backed out in front of me. I saw that the woman on the passenger side was wearing some kind of bandana on her head, much like you see the sports stars wearing on television under their football helmets. I followed them into town, down Main Street, where the man drove so slowly that it seemed he wanted to miss the green light. We stopped at two intersections and I got close enough to their car to see a Bible beside a blue umbrella on the shelf inside the rear window.

Exactly what the hell are you doing? I said to myself as I followed

147

them out of town. Just asking the question seemed to relieve me of any obligation to answer it. I felt the road open to me as we picked up speed. On the maple trees along the highway some of the leaves had already begun to redden. *All I'm going to do is find out how much money they'd pay,* I said out loud.

They pulled into a dirt parking lot out in front of a pale blue corrugated sheet metal building that looked like an auto body shop. At first I didn't see the white cross on the roof. I watched them come to a stop and then walk hand in hand toward the front door. I watched them disappear inside the church, and then I imagined them down on their knees praying inside the metal building. Praying that whoever had telephoned them, answering their advertisement, would call back.

That night Jack would not be consoled. The harder I tried, the harder he cried until I finally got into his bed and sang to him the "Edelweiss" song from *The Sound of Music.* When he finally calmed down I asked him what was wrong.

"I don't like the hole on your head," he said. His lower lip was quivering.

"Oh, Jackie boy," I said, "it's nothing. Look. Push the hair over it and it will go away." I leaned forward and aimed my bald spot at him. This only started him crying again. I pulled the covers up over us and held him tightly.

"Will you sleep with me?" he asked.

"Sure," I said.

"But I might pee on you."

"That's all right," I said. "I slept with you every night after Cara was born."

"Why?"

"Because she needed to be near the milk."

"Why?"

"Because she was as hungry as a bear all night long," I told him. "You peed on me every night, your pecker was always pointed in the wrong direction, right out the top of your diaper. I was always soaked by morning."

Jack laughed. "Sorry," he said.

"Don't be sorry," I said. "Someday when I'm old I'll ask you to sleep with me and I'll get you back."

I fell sound asleep. When I woke the lamp was on beside the bed. I found all of his plastic men lying there. Batman and Robin. The Lone Ranger. Indiana Jones. He had scraped the tops of their heads so that each of them had a bald spot like mine. This exquisite love, I thought, for a man who's willing to sell your new brother or sister to the highest bidder?

As I sat by his bed I heard Colleen out in the hallway. I wondered if she had found the columns of numbers I'd been writing inside the Yellow Pages of the Portland telephone directory, the front and back cover of the Century 21 multiple listing book, and even on page fourteen of Jack's *Curious George* bedtime book. I would read it slowly so that it put him to sleep, and then before I turned out his light I'd draw up another budget. It wasn't that I believed these budgets were suddenly going to reveal some truth about how we could salvage our future, but there was that marvelous instant when a kind of spiritual high would come as I divided the final figure by what I estimated it cost us to live each month, and there, before my eyes, the dollars would turn into *time*. How much time we had left to live on the money we had. How much time before Colleen stopped me in the hallway after all her children were asleep and asked me point blank if I was or was not going to continue to support her. How much time before I asked her if she was pregnant and what she wished for the baby's future.

The iron wheel rolling along its track — how much time before it stopped. How much time before I found out who I was.

The silent rushes of fear that I experienced also had to do with time. Checking a book out at the library one day I saw the return date of August 12, and I had to hold myself back from telling the woman in circulation that I wasn't going to be living in this town anymore by then, I would have run far away. And at an intersection watching a freight train pass, I pictured myself an older man riding in the boxcars like the hobos of my childhood, men who were no longer a burden to anyone.

In the mornings at first light I'd get up and prowl the house with a wet dish towel, looking for something to clean. Just as the sun struck the kitchen windows I would start polishing the table and chairs. Then I would make breakfast for the kids and hover over the table, taking away their dirty dishes and juice glasses the instant they were finished with them.

I spent one day setting our stuff out on the front lawn. I was putting up the yard sale sign when Colleen drove up the hill with the kids. I watched the station wagon slow down. Colleen took off her sunglasses and looked at what I'd done. Then she drove by and kept on going. She had Jack call me from her mother's house later to say they were eating dinner and spending the night there. He hung up before I could say anything.

I sat on the front steps of the house for a long time trying to come up with something I could say or do. It was late when I called Colleen. "Is your mother still awake," I asked her.

"We're just talking," she said.

"That's good," I said. "Do you think maybe you should ask her about us moving in with them?"

At first she didn't say anything. Then she told me that we

couldn't impose on her mother. "I want to come home," she said, "but first I want you to move everything back inside. Please."

I did. But then I decided that we were going to have to learn to manage in a one-bedroom apartment, and to prepare for this I moved the kids' beds and Cara's crib into our room one morning when everyone went to town.

Colleen can sleep through an attack of killer bees, and she took the change in stride while I lay awake most of the night listening to the kids breathe, cough, and roll over. Finally, remembering my visit with Billy, I plugged in a fan right next to my pillow. It made enough noise to keep me from waiting for the next little sound the kids would make, and I began sleeping well after that and looking forward to the morning light, when I could see everyone sleeping peacefully around me. Each night before they dropped off to sleep all the kids piled into our bed for a story. At first Colleen read to them from children's books she brought home from the library. Eventually I started taking over with homemade tales of the Great Depression, accounts of a fictional family that were based on stories my father had told me across the years. Because I had nothing else to do with my days, I devoted more and more time to developing these stories, and almost from the time I opened my eyes each morning I began looking forward to the end of the day when we were all together in bed.

When her mother volunteered to baby-sit one afternoon Colleen and I went to the beach together in Scarborough. We walked along the shore, past the spot where we had met, a mile or so beyond the beach houses, all the way to the most beautiful part of the shoreline, a private enclave called Prouts Neck. We ran into someone we knew there, a young man who Colleen had met years earlier and who was fond of her. He owned one of the big mansion houses at Prouts as well as a small cottage. I listened to him asking Colleen if we would be his guests at a dinner party he was throwing later in the week. Colleen accepted, and as soon as he walked away I laid into her. "You're just like your mother," I said. "Maybe it's a thing with Irishwomen. They marry working-class stiffs and spend their lives dreaming of a better life."

She looked down at the ground and shook her head slowly. Then she looked at me and said, "I'm not going to let you talk to me like that."

I watched her walk away. I sat down in the sand and felt sorry for myself for a while. I watched two old ladies in those awful skirt bathing suits rummaging the dunes. Both of them carried plastic trash bags that they were filling with driftwood and shells. They were having the time of their lives, and I thought how relieved some women must be when their husbands are dead and buried. These women looked like they had returned from a long, un-happy forced march that had taken everything from them except the precious little bit of time on their own that was left to them now.

I went back along the shore looking for Colleen. When I found her sitting in front of the flagpole, exactly where we had sat when we first met, the fight left me. I told her I was sorry, and then on the way up the path toward where our car was parked I took her hand and led her into the number seven stall in the row of bathhouses. She didn't say anything. She closed the door and leaned back against it. I could smell the sea heather and the sun-baked cedar planks beneath us. I kissed her and pulled her close with such force that her whole body stiffened in my hands. It was a strange moment, my passion for her and my rage running along the same edge.

Colleen looked frightened and pulled away. She told me that

she had been talking with the woman who worked at the little mom-and-pop store down the road from our house. "She's one of ten children. They all lived on a farm in northern Maine until they lost it in the Depression. The bank foreclosed on them. The only work that the father could find was in a ball bearings factory in Hartford, Connecticut, so they all moved there and stayed there until they had enough money to come back to Maine."

I knew what she was telling me. *That man,* that father, didn't turn out to be selfish and a coward. That was the kind of man I had always believed I was, and hadn't Colleen believed it too? And now if she had changed her mind about me was there anything I could do to restore myself in her eyes?

On the way home I stopped at the supermarket to buy a six-pack of beer and a new bottle for Cara. I got sidetracked into the produce section, where I watched an employee, a man about my age, spraying the lettuce with cold water. He had on a green apron and a hair net. I was wondering if he had kids at home and if he was careful never to wear the hair net home so that his kids didn't see him with it on. Maybe each time he put it on at the beginning of his shift he reminded himself that he was working to put food on the table and shoes on his kids' feet. Or maybe he just spent the money foolishly on the things he saw advertised on television. The way he attended to the lettuce and then the celery with such care made me think that he was a thoughtful man who, if he was given a raise, would spend the extra money for things that were not advertised on TV; he would spend it for piano lessons for his kids. I made up a budget for him and tried to figure out how he made ends meet. If he was paid six dollars an hour for a forty-hour work week and his wife earned the same, then their gross income was $480 a week. After taxes, maybe $400, times four: $1,600.00 a month. His rent or mortgage payment had to be at least $600 a month. If he had a car payment, that would run him another $200. A second car for his wife to get to her job? $200 more. Gas to run them, $100 a month. Electricity $100. Heating fuel $200. Food would put them over the line.

I was watching him and thinking that he probably was allowed to take his hair net off when he worked out back in the warehouse unpacking crates of vegetables. Then, out of the corner of my eye, I saw someone looking at me. He was a neatly dressed old man, with a bald head ringed by a halo of white hair. But in his surprising, blue eyes I saw a young man I had known more than twenty-five years earlier and I recognized him just as he figured out who I was, and we were both caught in the shock of recognition and then the crushing wave of sadness, both of us thinking the same thing — *Oh no, not you too!*

"Jesus, it's good to see you," I said.

"You too," he said. "It's good to see you too."

"You look good," I said.

"You look good too."

When he told me that he was living on Scarborough beach in one of the big condominums, I was immediately seized by a sense of well-being. Fate! Nearly thirty years before, when I was seventeen years old, he was manager of the summer hotel when I went for my first job interview. He hired me on the spot to wash dishes. In my life of good jobs and bad jobs, he was the best boss I ever had, a man who was positively masterful at earning his employees' devotion. I worked for him three summers, and after we'd lost touch he had gone on to become a wealthy and highly respected businessman in Maine.

We talked our way through the checkout line, out the door, and to his car. His kids were off at boarding school and he had time on his hands and he seemed eager to get together. "Some day Colleen and I will come by with the kids," I told him.

"Good," he said. "That would be good."

I guess I made more of it than I should have. Driving home, I began by telling Colleen how frightening it was to see him looking so old, and then I talked myself through that to the hopeful possibility that he was just the right person to talk to about a job because he would have all sorts of important contacts in the business world and he was a man who had once judged me worthy of employment.

Colleen listened patiently.

I said I was going to stop at the mall for some new clothes. "Want to come with me?"

She didn't. She said she was eager to get home, to relieve her mom. "Why do you need new clothes?" she asked with a worried expression.

"Well, I don't really," I said, "except that I guess I still believe that the right tweed jacket and a blue oxford button-down shirt and a pair of penny loafers can make a difference."

She laughed at me gently and said, "You don't really believe that."

"Why not?" I said. "You don't think that I can still make an impression?"

"It's not that."

"What is it, then?"

"I don't know. It's just that we don't have money to spend on new clothes," she said.

I spent it anyway. Almost $450 in less than an hour on the shirt, the tweed sport jacket, the shoes, and a new belt. The mall was crowded with shoppers that included a few people like me trying hard to believe they could be *anything* in the right clothes.

The next morning I walked the beach in my new clothes to try and make Dino see that I deserved better than what had been happening to me lately. I stopped and reached down for a sand dollar that was being swept in on the surf. I was going to give it to Colleen when I got home. When my hand went below the water I felt something sting me, and when I pulled my hand out of the surf blood was running down my wrist from where I'd been caught by an ungodly looking fishing lure shaped like a cucumber with three sets of hooks hanging from it. I was dazed for a moment and as I stood there the sea advanced and soaked my new shoes and socks. I bent down and held my hand in the water to try and stop the bleeding. By then I had blood on the breast pocket of the new tweed jacket, and if I'd gone the rest of the way to Dino's door I was sure I would have looked to him more like the survivor of a shipwreck than a candidate for employment. Maybe a man who might some day wear a hair net to work. I started back home.

Colleen was waiting for me in the kitchen. I handed her the sand dollar. "It's all I've got," I said miserably. "Do you know how to get blood out of wool?"

I hit bottom that week in the living room of the Christian couple's house. Colleen had gone into Portland one morning to look into the requirements to receive food stamps and fuel assistance. When she got back with the car I told her that I was going to take Cara to ride the mechanical horse in front of Kmart. To reinforce this lie I emptied the change bowl on the kitchen counter and took all the quarters.

We stopped at LaVerdier's drugstore on Route 1, where I bought a box of Magic Markers. I opened them on the front seat.

"Daddy only needs the blue one," I said to Cara. "The rest of these are yours." I handed her the box and she drew all over her car seat while I worked on my tweed sport coat until I had covered all the blood with pale blue lines that blended into the wool.

I was going to ask the Christian couple for twenty-five thousand dollars. I wasn't going to lie to them, and I wasn't going to beat around the bush either. And I wasn't going to feel bad about this because we already had four beautiful childen and they didn't have any, and selling them a baby would give us the money to survive for a year until there was a whole new round of college teaching jobs to apply for.

They had a white living room. Cream colored is what it was, I guess. Four cream-colored couches pushed up to the sides of a square, glass-topped table in the center of the room. I was watching the lady stir her coffee. I was just looking at her thin wrists and thinking that she must have some health problem that kept her from conceiving. I was going to tell her that I needed to be well compensated because I had lost my job and my prospects for another were very poor. I heard her husband say, "Oh, no, sweetheart, you don't want to do that." When I looked up, the lady was reaching for Cara, but it was too late. She had taken the orange Magic Marker and drawn a big lopsided circle on one of the couches.

On the way home, I stopped at the mall. "My wife gets so angry at me," I told the clerk. "Every time my birthday is coming up, I go out and buy something for myself and then it turns out that she's bought the same thing." I don't know whether she believed me or not, but she never noticed the bloodstain beneath the blue Magic Marker. She took the coat back and gave me a full refund of $239 and I was very grateful.

Over the days that followed I negotiated with the couple by

telephone. The lady felt awful. She said it was her fault, that she had planned to have all four couches Scotchgarded but had been busy with a church project and hadn't gotten around to it. Each couch cost twelve hundred dollars, and in the end we agreed to split the cost. I paid them in cash so there wouldn't be any trace of the transaction. I drove all the way back alone. When she came to the door she had on a neck brace and her hair was in a bun that lay on her shoulder like a sleeping cat.

"I feel terrible about this," she said.

"It's okay," I told her. "My wife only buys the Magic Markers that wash off. It was my fault." I thought briefly about telling her that if she were to get the baby she wanted so badly, once he or she turned two they would have no mercy for her white couches. Then I looked past her in the doorway to the empty rooms behind her. I thought about the awful quiet in those rooms, a stillness that was always there and that never changed. I thought about how, late in the evening, after waiting all day for people to call and answer her newspaper advertisement, she might listen to her own footsteps on the quiet floors and think she was losing her mind in the terrible stillness. I wondered if families had lived in those rooms over the years before she became the owner and if from time to time she ran across little signs of their existence that tormented her. I thought for sure that it was her husband's idea to collect cash from me for the damaged couch; like me, he was scared about his money. I told her that I was sorry. "Yes," she said sadly. I turned and walked to my car, expecting her to call to me to ask if I still wanted to talk about arrangements for the baby. But she didn't and when I glanced back, the front door was closed. All the way home and for several days I thought of her down on her knees inside the sheet metal church praying for the chance to be a mother, and checking the newspaper each morning to see that her advertisement appeared. I dreamed about her, always the same dream; she summons me and I make love to her over and over until she finally conceives. The trouble all along was her husband, but she was forbidden by her religion to have sex with another man. She makes love to me in a room festooned with religious artifacts. Plaster of Paris praying hands on the bedside table, Jesus on the cross above the headboard of the bed. A clock with each of the twelve disciples standing in for the numbers. Following the instructions of her pastor she pretends that I am her husband.

Like those little nesting Russian dolls, this dream kept opening to new versions of itself throughout each night, and for the first time in my life I couldn't sleep. After a week of this I went to a doctor, who gave me a prescription for sleeping pills. They worked so well, casting me into a depthless rest, that I began taking them every day at noon as well. Just as the theme music for *Gilligan's Island* began I was already slipping away into a slumber that usually lasted until supper. I craved the sleep these pills provided and one night when I was particularly anxious about the fact that Erin's front teeth were coming in crooked I took five of the pills, hoping to sleep through the night and the next day. I was sitting on the couch with Colleen about an hour after I took the pills. She got up to go into another room and something powerful told me that if I didn't get into bed I was going to fall onto the floor. Once I lay down flat the room began spinning around. I could hear Colleen asking me what was wrong over and over again. Finally I asked her to turn on the light, and when she did, I saw a flash, but other than that I couldn't see a thing. I reached across the bed and shook her arm. "Call an ambulance," I said, "but tell them not to come with the siren on. Please."

The whole time they were putting in the IV, I kept asking

them to please be quiet so they didn't wake the kids. The hinges on the iron stretcher snapped loudly into place and I had this awful picture of Cara standing up in her crib and watching as they wheeled me past her room.

I spent one night on a hospital ward with people who had tried to kill themselves and were heavily drugged. In the morning we were led to chairs in one corner of the room to watch a television that was bolted to the wall. The female host of a talk show was interviewing fat women married to men who accused them of turning into cows after they had their first baby.

I got out of there as fast as I could. Colleen had her mom watch the kids so she could pick me up by herself. When I called her to set the time, I asked her to please throw my baseball bat and balls in the back of the car.

We didn't say much on the way home. I told her that I had spoken with the doctor on the telephone and he was waiting for me to come by his office. "He said he'd forgotten to get my signature on some release form," I said to Colleen.

"Did you tell him it was only an accident?"

"Yeah. Sure. Did you put the bat and balls in back?"

She nodded. "Are you going to the Little League field today?"

I was aware that it would scare her in some way or confirm what she had feared if I told her I didn't really want to see the kids today and that all I could imagine doing was hitting balls at the field, but I told her this anyway, and the concern in her voice reassured me that I still knew her well enough to predict certain responses.

"Any mail?" I asked.

She shook her head. "Do you want to do anything special today?"

"Why?"

"It's your birthday," she said.

I spent most of it at the ball field. I was hoping the businessman would be there because I wanted to ask him to tell me the craziest things he had done when he went off the rails. Instead I fell asleep for three hours in center field. I woke up in a thunderstorm and I knew Colleen would be driving to the field to get me, so I started walking on the back roads through town. I got about halfway when I was overcome by the desire to get a job before the day was through. A job that offered health insurance in case I collapsed and got to the point where I couldn't get out of bed.

The first place I came to was the Shop & Save supermarket. I went up to the service counter and asked a young man in pleated trousers and a tie if they needed any bag boys. "I'm on leave from my teaching job," I lied, "and I thought it would be fun to work a few hours here every week."

He put an application on the counter in front of me and started going over it while I read through it madly, trying to find the part that told about insurance benefits.

"So, where were you teaching?" I heard him ask. Then it hit me. My God he's going to want to call Colgate University. The administration and faculty would be back from summer vacation by now and word would get around that I was working as a bag boy and this would be the end of the dean's recommendation.

"Well," I stammered — and I was about to lie again when I remembered that I was wearing my hat that said "Colgate Football" across the front. I was dead.

Or maybe it only said "Red Raider Football"? Maybe. I couldn't be sure without taking off my hat and reading the front of it, and I couldn't do anything so obvious. I felt like I had during the final stages of drunken college card games when, invariably, we played that stupid game — Indian Poker, I think it was

161

called — where you took a card from the deck and without looking at it held it against your forehead for everyone else to see what
you were betting on except you. I felt my legs going numb. All I
wanted to ask the guy was how many bags of groceries I had to
carry out to the parking lot before the medical benefits kicked in.
He waited patiently and I tried in vain to improvise. Finally I
picked up the application and told him it was really for my oldest
daughter.

As the last days of August had begun to turn cool I was overcome
by a desire to return to a college campus. It was the time of the
year that had always felt like a beginning, a fresh start full of
promise and hope. I was watching the late news on television one
night and when they showed football players arriving for
preseason drills at the University of Maine, where I had once
taught, it took me like a fever. The next morning I drove to the
campus. I watched the team work out and then walked through
all the buildings to each of the rooms where I had held my classes.

When I got home it was late and I was hanging my head like a
defeated prizefighter. Colleen came downstairs and told me that
there wasn't going to be a new baby. At first I thought that I
hadn't heard her correctly. Then I was surprised and then my
relief overpowered my surprise, and after that I couldn't look into
her eyes anymore; whenever she would look into mine I would
turn my head away. I tried to make her smile by recalling her
mother's story about how she had miscarried three times trying
for the first child, and then finally she had gone to the nuns at St.
John's rectory and they had blessed her womb. After that came
five healthy babies in the space of six years.

I smiled at her, but she looked so sad that I felt guilty for
smiling. I pictured her in her nightgown, sitting on the cold toilet

seat, me a hundred miles away from where I should have been, down on my knees beside her, holding her hand. I thought of the children waking in the night and wondering why their mother was crying. I wanted to put my arms around her, but I felt unworthy of that.

I told her how sorry I was. I thought, *Where does this end?*

"Why did you go?" she asked.

At first I didn't understand. "*Where?*" I asked.

"Up to the university," she said.

I looked at her long enough to see that she had allowed herself to wonder if maybe I was going to surprise her now by revealing that there was a job at the university and that I had gone to see about it. I shook my head no, and then watched her turn away. I felt disoriented, the way you feel coming out of a matinee, stepping into darkness where there had been light before.

11

Clothes $448.72. Food $311.78. Tires for car $66.00.
Food $249.00. Electricity $61.20. Telephone $37.65.
Refund for sport coat $239.00. Couch $600.00.
Miscellaneous $112.30.

                    B A L A N C E *September 1, 1993: $3,515.75*

I know that it takes a very weak man to lose his way when he has a beautiful wife and four healthy children living under his roof, no debt, over three thousand dollars left in the bank, and he's not in a war or facing anything even close to real peril, but I was so lost over the whole next year of my life that I could never look at Colleen without setting off this amazing image in my head that had her living with another man and working at the drive-through window of a bank in town where I would be the first customer every weekday morning, waiting there, just staring at the glass when she raised the curtain to open for business.

All of which is to say that after sending out thirty-four more job letters that autumn and being rejected by all of them over the winter I lost track of the next year of my life. The day-to-day matters are unclear to me because Colleen took care of all of them. She found us a house to rent for the year, got the kids enrolled in their new schools, packed their lunches every day, and bought their clothes with her own money. That is, the money she brought in each week by filling the house with other peoples' children, whom she cared for as if they were our own. I never learned their names or talked with their mothers and fathers because I quarantined myself in an upstairs room, where I sailed away my days on sleeping pills and then prowled the house for food and mail at night when all was still. At the children's bedtime Colleen would send them to call hello to me through the closed door. Jack always came around dusk. He would scratch on the door and call to me, "Daddy? It's me, Jack." And I would feel like I had already left him behind and that he was calling to someone else, someone he would introduce me to someday when he was all grown up.

I don't think I made a conscious decision to surrender this way. It just came on sometime in the winter when it became clear to me that I wasn't going to find a decent job. I had received canned rejection letters from everywhere, including two community colleges in Idaho and California, which in better days I wouldn't have tried for. Just before my final rejection my eyes were opened when I answered the distress signal of a former student who had been dumped from a graduate program in theater for missing too many classes. He asked me if I would intervene on his behalf and so I telephoned the dean and pleaded his case. The dean listened for a while before he told me that there were no conditions under which he would reverse his decision. "Listen," he replied. "He may be a wonderful person and a great actor but we have a policy about class attendance and it's very strict because, the point is, we don't *need* any more actors, there are already too many great actors, there are hundreds of them in line for every part."

Those words — *We don't need any more actors.* I surrendered to those words, knowing that they were true, they were the words that would write the future of America. And they meant that we didn't need any more college professors either. And no more doctors or lawyers. No more of anything that entitled one to a grand life. There were too many people, too many talented and driven people waiting at every slot for a way in. Some of these people had fought their way from a hopeless beginning to get there; they were resourceful and tough as nails. Some of them would fight viciously just for standing room outside the door. One of the last things I did before I collapsed was argue with Bradford about this. I told him what the businessman at the Little League field had said to me, that someday the downtrodden and the humiliated were going to come screaming into the yacht clubs and the country clubs and the tennis clubs and the prep schools and the Ivy League colleges and they were going to put a knife at the throats of our children and say, "Ante up, you motherfuckers. You've had it too good for too long!"

I told my friend that we were spoiled just because *we had the chance* to work for the good things. "And these people who've had nothing," I said, "are much tougher than we are. Once they decide to come and claim their chance, they'll eat guys like you and me for breakfast. You remember struggling to get through medical school, but I'm telling you that was a piece of cake compared to what these people have been through. You always had a safety net beneath you. Hell, I remember your father's credit card in the glove compartment of your old Buick. There was someone behind you to pick you up if things got rough."

It got to the point where I didn't talk with Bradford anymore. When he or anyone else called, Colleen told them I was taking a nap.

My sole contribution to the operation of the family was that I did the grocery shopping every Friday at the new, glistening Shop & Save store in Scarborough. Here was the gallery in which America's finest exhibitions of marketing and productivity were on display, and I wandered up and down the mirrored aisles like an immigrant who couldn't understand a word of the written language. All the brightly packaged products seemed connected in a single dizzying montage, seamless and brilliant, that made me forget what Colleen had sent me shopping for. I fell prey to the clever gimmicks and could not keep from buying all two-for-the-price-of-ones, no matter what they were. I read the promotional copy, believing every printed word was a solemn promise. I chose products for their packaging, hopeful that the bright colors would pierce the darkness of my home and light our way back to a meaningful existence. At the checkout lanes it sometimes took all my powers of self-possession to keep from trembling before the cashier and just walking away from my loaded cart.

During this time, without saying anything to me, Colleen stayed in touch with my former student Billy. Just after Christmas his life blew up again and he was readmitted to the psychiatric clinic at Yale New Haven Hospital, where he was treated for clinical depression and obsessive-compulsive behavior. He was released after a month, and he asked if he could come live with us until he got his feet back on the ground. Colleen fixed up a room for him in the basement. I found her hanging the kids' artwork on the walls the night before Billy arrived. I asked her if she was sure that this was a wise thing to do. "You'll have one nut living above you, and another down below," I said.

She ignored this and told me that the girls were old enough now to learn something from helping take care of Billy. "They can read to him," she said. "And he can walk them to the bus. I'm thinking about Erin, really. She's becoming too self-centered. I won't let my children turn out to be the kind of people who think their lives are more important than anyone else's."

"Like me," I said.

"I didn't say that."

Billy arrived with his clothes in one brown paper bag and his books and pills in another. He was taking 300 mg of lithium, 425 mg of desipramine, 275 mg of Zoloft, and a sedative each day, and for the first few weeks he was with us he spoke of nothing but his medication and his mental illness, and he only left the basement to get glasses of apple juice to cool the burning in his throat caused by the pills and to go into Portland for his twice-weekly appointments with a psychiatrist at the Maine Medical Center. Colleen wouldn't let him drive; she drove him herself. Then, gradually, her prescription began to work; the kids dragged their toys and books down into the basement day after day until they finally managed one rainy afternoon to drag Billy back upstairs with them. He became absorbed into their busy lives and grew stronger, and it wasn't terribly long before he was the Billy he had been as a college student. He began spending a lot of time in the library in town and he signed on for volunteer work at the homeless shelter. Just before Easter he was hired in the middle of the semester by a private school in southern Connecticut to teach English to students with learning disabilities. Before he left he told me that he had been reading the short stories of Raymond Carver to the residents of the shelter and that the people there were very grateful. "I know that you miss teaching," he said to me, "and I know that the people there are eager to learn."

"What can *I* teach them, Billy?" I asked.

"Whatever's important to you," he said. "The only thing you have to remember is that they want the truth. They've heard so much bullshit in their lives that they don't have much tolerance for it."

I laughed. "Hell, Billy," I said to him, "bullshit was my stock in trade. Don't you remember?"

He smiled at me and said, "You were the best teacher I ever had."

I was still down for the count when the following summer ended, not having worked a day or earned a cent since I taught my last class at Colgate. I was dreading another round of job applications when the professional journals would begin advertising positions again in mid-September. And though I had given up standing in line at the job center months before, I was keeping track of the balance in our checkbook, and telling myself that when the last of our money was gone, I would go out and find some kind of work. By Labor Day we had just over two thousand dollars left. During the eleven months I spent lying in bed, Colleen had kept us afloat, and on her own she also made arrangements for us to rent a seaside cottage for the winter on her favorite beach, just half a mile from where we had met ten years before.

A joke in Maine, borrowed from Ross Perot's campaign rant against American businesses heading to Mexico, has it that by noon on Labor Day in Maine there is a great sucking sound at the interstate toll booths as the summer tourists leave.

At exactly noon on Labor Day we arrived at the beach house at

Prouts Neck like a caravan of drifters and gypsies, Colleen leading the way with our rusted station wagon stuffed to the roof, me following in a U-Haul truck just ahead of Colleen's sister and brother-in-law and their three kids, then her father and mother, who had lived for forty years just seven miles from Prouts Neck but had never set foot beyond the electronic security gate. Our landlord had notified the private police force, so we all waved jauntily to the cop who was waiting at the end of Garrison Lane. He didn't wave back, and as I passed him in the truck this picture came into my head that scared the shit out of me — the cop is in his uniform, stepping inside our rented cottage some dark night this winter, knocking the snow off his boots and gazing into the living room, where Colleen and the kids are weeping, and he is reminding himself that he *knew for certain* when he first saw us arriving like refugees on Labor Day that there was going to be trouble.

I was aware from the start that this cottage by the sea on the beach where we had met was Colleen's gift to me and our children. She made all the arrangements on her own and I felt very much like I was just following her the way the children were. At one end of our lane, just across the main road, was a magnificent private golf course laid out along the shore with a dozen tennis courts hidden below tall evergreens, and a yacht club and docks inside the cove. At the other end of the lane, a few hundred feet from our cottage, was a five-mile stretch of sand and dunes, ledges and cliffs practically unpopulated all the way to the lighthouse at Cape Elizabeth.

As it turned out, we arrived before the summer renters had departed. Colleen had the good sense to pass our driveway, where a man in red pants stood smoking a cigarette next to his tan Mercedes coupe. We all pulled onto the side of the lane, beyond a tall hedge. By now the kids were too excited to contain, and when Erin opened her door, a frying pan and two pots rolled onto the ground. I saw the man in our driveway turn lazily and glare at us. I imagined him calling to his wife, "Come on, Bunny, you can finish your makeup in the car. Let's get out of here before the common people start introducing themselves!"

Colleen came up alongside me. "I feel like the Joads," I said to her.

She took my hand. "It's so pretty here," she said. "Let's be happy here."

The kids and their cousins went flying inside through the front door of the house before the blinking turn signal on the Mercedes had disappeared at the end of the lane. I walked the boundaries by myself, pleased to discover that the handsome cottages bordering ours were already closed up for the winter. I hung a clothesline across the courtyard in back and this task lifted my spirits surprisingly.

We cooked out on the grill on the deck and had a big family picnic supper that went on until the mosquitoes ran us inside. I built a fire in the living room and played cribbage with Colleen's dad. The kids kept running into the room to report their exciting discoveries around the house, and I listened to Colleen's mother asking, "Now where does *that* door go?"

"It's a great house," Colleen's father said to me. "Imagine cooking a big meal in such a beautiful kitchen."

"Thanksgiving," I said. "Let's have it out here." He agreed. I watched his big hands shuffling the cards and for a few seconds I imagined he was counting out hundred-dollar bills to loan us. He was a handsome, rugged Irishman who lost his father at age sixteen and gave up the chance to go to college so he could help provide for his younger brother and sisters. He had been working ever since. For the last thirty-nine years he walked the Texaco docks at night where the oil tankers tied up. It was brutally cold and lonely work. For overtime pay when he was raising his family he had worked double shifts on all the holidays, and Colleen remembered accompanying her mother and her five brothers and sisters to take him his Christmas dinner at the docks. A man who guarded his private thoughts so intensely that his life was a secret even to those who knew him best, he nevertheless was a consummate neighborhood man who would shovel the widow's driveway after a blizzard or do the grocery shopping for the single mother too ill with the flu to go out herself, always without being asked and always too shy to stick around to be thanked. A solid man with a marvelous simplicity of heart, John McQuinn shrugged off the rhapsodies and the vulgarities of American culture. He traveled light, acquiring only the things that he needed. He remained content across the years living in the same house, holding down the same job, and staying married to the same woman.

The only thing he had said to me about my situation since we returned to Maine was that for most of his working life when he heard that a man was out of work it was a rare thing, and now he could name twenty-five or thirty men who had lost their jobs in the last year. Whatever he thought of the way I was raising his grandchildren, providing for his daughter or conducting myself, he kept to himself.

"How much oil do you think we'll burn here this winter?" I asked him.

He looked around. I told him that there was no insulation in the walls or ceilings. He got a pained look on his face. "Eight or nine gallons a day," he said. "Around there anyway. More if the burner is real old. You should have it checked."

At a dollar forty a gallon that was almost ninety bucks a week.

"If you buy two or three cords of firewood," he went on, "you could close off all these doors and keep this one room warm with the fireplace." This was the closest he would ever come to telling another man how to live his life, but when he raised his eyes from the cribbage board and looked at me I could tell that he was hoping I would take his advice.

I watched him walk across the room and check the flue on the chimney. Suddenly I wanted to know what he thought of me being at home every day, not having a job to go to. I wanted to know if I was fulfilling some prediction he had made to himself the first time I showed up at his house, a thirty-one-year-old man coming to pick up his twenty-year-old daughter. But I had never been able to read him at all, and I couldn't tell what he was thinking tonight.

"Papa!" Jack yelled to him. "We got cable TV!"

"Hooray!" he called to Jack. When he sat down again at the cribbage board he picked up his cards and smiled. "The kids are going to be happy out here," he said. "That's what counts."

He had to leave early to get some sleep before work, but he didn't want to break up the party so he left the car for Nanny to come home later and I gave him a ride into South Portland. There he would take his nap in the red stuffed chair in his living room, like he did every night before he went to work at midnight with the lunch his wife made for him to eat at three in the morning.

He got out of the car, thanked me for the ride, and then stood in the driveway for a minute just sort of looking down the street of tiny, working-class houses stacked in rows. It could have been a street anywhere in America where, side by side, matching homes were built to accommodate the soldiers returning from the Second World War. "I don't know when it started," I heard John say, "but it used to be that this place was teeming with life. Now I come home from work in the morning and it's like a ghost town. Both parents are already at work, the kids are at day care . . . Big, busy lives, you know? A lot of debt to the banks. Everybody used to have six or seven kids in these houses, two or three kids sharing each bedroom. Now you look around — there's only one or two kids in each family, but there's hardly a house on the street where they haven't added on an extra room, enlarged the kitchen, or knocked out the roof for gables. And two cars in every driveway. All of that costs too much money. The banks are happy to lend it to you. They'll keep loaning you more money right up to the point where you put the rope around the rafters to hang yourself. There's nothing wrong with learning to live with less. If you can close your eyes to all this and learn not to need so much, you'll be better off in the long run."

I got back to the cottage in time to help give the kids baths in the big old-fashioned tub on the second floor. All four of them still fit in the tub at the same time. Colleen sat on the floor admiring them. Jack's thatch of snow white hair. Erin's deep green eyes. The red in Nell's hair. And Cara's tiny feet. I saw Colleen's smile drop away and I knew what she was thinking. "If we get some good news in this house," I whispered in her ear, "we can have another baby."

She didn't look at me. "Thank you," she said softly. She gazed at the children and went on. "Just think how lucky we are to have them." Jack stood up, flexed his muscles, and let out a Tarzan screech. "Sit down," Colleen said calmly. "If I hadn't had them, what would life be like?"

I told her that she would always have them, no one could ever take them away from her. She got up and took a stack of towels from a shelf. "Come on, you guys, time for bed. The school bus comes at seven-forty-five."

There was a guest room attached to the garage, quarters for live-in summer help. When I found a couch there that pulled out into a double bed, I dragged it into the living room, across from the fireplace. I unfolded it and put on Colleen's favorite flannel sheets while she was taking her bath. I lit a candle on the mantel and opened all the windows to let the salt air in. The white lace curtains blew like sails. You could hear the waves running onto the shore and you could smell the salty warmth of the long summer in the wood walls. I waited a long time for Colleen to come back downstairs, and then I found her sleeping with Nell. There was a worried expression on her face, and I thought about waking her to tell her that she had done well getting us all through the past year and finding the way back to this beach. She was like her father, she didn't need much to be content.

After a while I went outside. The stars were bright along the shore where I had first met Colleen. From the first hour we were drawn together by a powerful physical desire that came naturally for twelve years, until the past year, when making love to Colleen required that I first persuade her that I was still the person who used to wait for her on the beach until she came down from the hotel in her white chambermaid's uniform to lie next to me while her morning's tips spilled out of her pockets like silver into the sand.

When I got back to the cottage I went into the guest room attached to the garage and turned on the overhead light. There was a director's chair, a wicker lamp, and a table that would serve as a desk. It looked to me like the perfect place to set up my office. I thought about how I would walk from here to the mailbox every day at noon to check for replies from colleges. Maybe I would get a map of the United States and hang it on another wall and put straight pins in it to mark where I had applied for college teaching jobs. I could buy pins with different-colored heads to mark the various stages I was passing through in the application process. I looked around the room, deciding where I could put shelves for my books. When I remembered that I had taken all my books to the dump in Yarmouth twelve months before, I felt a disorienting lightness in my head. I just stood in the room without moving. I saw that the door had a lock on it and for some reason this satisfied a nameless fear or desire. I thought about what I would do in this room and how much I needed to be alone here.

The next day I went through our boxes until I found my old leather attaché case. I set it on the table, and next to it my wallet and a carefully folded map of the United States. These three things — map, attaché, and wallet — represented to me my return to the ranks of respectable men, and several times each day I would stop in the room and rearrange them on the top of the table and then pause before them like a shrine and touch each of them once more before I locked the door and went out.

The first days of autumn were clement and I spent them exploring our new surroundings with Jack. Each morning we would put Erin and Nell on the bus at seven-forty-five, wave goodbye, then walk off with our heads down because we started missing them the moment the bus pulled away. I'd lift him up onto my shoulders and hike half a mile along the beach to the Black Point Inn, where the nice woman at the front desk sold us a *Boston Globe.* Then we'd sit on the rocks and I'd read aloud about the pennant races in both leagues and the early reports from hockey training camps. We always stopped at the big shorefront houses and peered in the windows at the furniture that caretakers had covered with sheets. I made up stories for Jack about the owners of these houses who had returned to the great cities of the East, leaving behind the empty rooms that looked like stage sets of summer stock theaters. I told him that there was food and gold in the cupboards and that when it got to be winter we were going to drive into Portland and round up all the homeless people and bring them to these empty houses. "How will we get in?" he asked me.

"Well," I said, "how would Batman get in?"

He thought for a second. "Magic," he said.

"We'll use magic, then," I told him.

"Do we still have magic?" he asked hopefully.

I tried to prove it by building a fort in the branches of the pine tree next to our garage. We spent most of a week gathering wood on the beach and we were running his pirate flag up on a rope and a pulley the morning a man stepped into view below us. The minute I saw him, I knew we were in trouble. "You built your tree house in my tree," he said.

I felt my heart begin to race. "This is your tree?" I said.

"Yes, it is," he said.

I looked around. "That's your house?"

"That's my *headache*," he said.

I climbed down and apologized. "We're just here for the winter," I said. "Would it be all right if we took it down next spring?"

"No" was all he said.

I began taking the fort apart while he watched. He went home and continued watching from his deck until I had carted away all the lumber.

"We don't have a fort now," Jack said to me. He was pissed.

"Come on, Batman," I said to him.

"I'm not Batman. I'm Robin — *you're* Batman!"

He started crying. He followed me into the guest room and I forgot about him while I ran my hands over the attaché case, the map, and the wallet.

"Mommy said we can't turn the heat on," he said.

I turned and looked at him. "Why not?" I said.

He shrugged his shoulders. "Because we're poor."

I knelt down beside him. "Why are we poor?"

"Because you got fired."

"Well," I said, "we're not going to be cold, because we're all going to sleep in the living room right in front of the fire, okay?"

I watched his eyes light up. "Can we keep the cable too?" he asked.

Those first days in our new home I began getting up early, shaving and taking a shower, putting on a shirt and tie, then marching off to the guest room like anybody else going to an office to work. Thirty-three colleges advertised openings in their English departments, and I worked all day every day writing letters and putting together copies of my dossier. Just the routine of this work was enough to drown my old fears in new hope, and when the girls came home from school each day we all did something together as a family. We raided the gardens abandoned by the summer people, had picnics at the private beach club, and took long bicycle rides right past the NO BICYCLES sign on the wooden ramp that ran through the bird sanctuary. We were living in one of the most beautiful places on earth and I wanted us to act as if we owned it.

12

In the *Boston Globe* each morning that au-
tumn there were accounts of a ten-year-old girl abducted from
her home and strangled in the dead of night while her family
slept, a Catholic cardinal under investigation for sexual abuse, a
sixteen-year-old-boy on trial after murdering a classmate for his
hooded sweatshirt, an eminent cardiologist charged with siphon-
ing $4 million from a nonprofit research laboratory in order to
purchase modern art and a mansion to hang it in. It was just more
of the same, I suppose, the battering ram of disillusionment that
people try to dodge all day long and then barricade themselves
against at night with locked doors and rented movies. But one
morning after I started a fire with the hopeless help wanted pages
that told triumphantly of the versatility of American workers laid
off from their jobs at the auto plant but now blissfully retrained to
be guards at federal prisons, I looked across the room at Jack
sitting an inch from the TV screen watching *Lassie*. It was just a

moment, but I suddenly felt certain that something was being taken from us — something that was a lot bigger than a job or money.

"Get your boots and coat on, buster" I said to Jack, "and let's get out of here."

He thought we were going to the beach, where, for the past few days, we'd been cutting the netting out of lobster traps carried in from the cove on the tides and sewing them together for a hockey goal we were building in the garage. When I turned my back to the ocean he shouted, "You're going the wrong way, Daddy." I stopped and looked at him in his five-year-old glory, a thatch of white hair, his rubber boots on the wrong feet, jelly from his toast at the corners of his mouth. I laughed out loud and swung him off the ground and up onto my shoulders. We walked to the end of the lane, crossed the main road, crawled on our bellies under the wire fence, and entered the woods that surrounded the private golf course. "We have to be real quiet," I said to him. I was nervous. "You lead the way," I said. We passed four POSITIVELY NO TRESPASSING signs and crawled under another fence before we got our first clear view of the fairway. It was a marvelous golf course and the rich people who owned it had named the holes the way they named their summer cottages. Names like Old Home, The Dunes, The Marshes. The grass was so green it looked like it had been lacquered, and lining both sides of the fairway for as far as we could see were thousands of giant Norway spruces reaching to the identical height in the sky. Beyond the trees there was the ocean. There was nothing for Jack to look at, nothing but the breathtaking beauty of the place, until two golf carts, tiny white boxes against the low blue sky, appeared in the distance. "There," I whispered to him. "Don't make a sound." They moved silently along the fairway like boats gliding across an emerald lake. They came straight toward us. I watched Jack staring out at them.

The golfers parked their carts close enough to us so we could smell their cigar smoke and hear them talking. I had my arm around Jack. We were lying flat on the ground, facedown in the brush and pine needles. I waited until all four men had hit their balls, then I lifted my head enough to see a pair of yellow trousers walk past. I put my hand over Jack's mouth, and when he looked into my eyes with fear I made a funny face to reassure him.

After they had gone we crawled out of the woods, emerging on the tee like wary survivors of some battle. I let Jack work the ball washer a few times while I kept a lookout and then we called it a day and went home.

A few days later, we were back on the golf course. We discovered a small stone marker in the ground near the ninth tee. Before I could read the bronze sentences inscribed on it, a foursome came over the rise in the fairway. I dove straight into the woods and Jack dove on top of me, laughing with delight. We watched a fat man in a pale blue beret hit his ball deep into the woods and then drop a second ball without his partners seeing him and hit it straight down the fairway and pretend he hadn't hit the first one. "The guy with the fat butt is cheating," I whispered. "Don't ever cheat or you'll look as pathetic as Mr. Fat Butt."

They were still more than two hundred yards from us, heading slowly toward the green when I took Jack's hand and we started running through the woods. I figured we would beat the golfers to the green by a few minutes and maybe we'd get lucky and find a ball. We did. We found three, in fact, and I had time to throw one onto the green just a few feet from the hole. We hid again and it was pure joy listening to the four golfers trying to figure out where the ball had come from and which of them had cheated by hitting an extra ball.

That's how it began, as fun. We discovered right away that most of the people who play golf cheat at it, and their antics are hilarious to observe. I don't think that I had subversion in mind; it was just the chance to laugh again. God, it was funny to see a grown man swing for all he was worth and hit a ball so poorly that it just dribbled a few feet in front of his spiked shoes.

The next day Jack and I returned to the stone marker. I read him the bronze writing: *Here on June 24, 1713, Josiah Hunniwell, the great Indian fighter, and eighteen men were killed by Indians in a surprise attack.* Before we went home for supper we made two bows and ten good arrows in honor of the Indians who had been killed on the golf course, rather than the white men whose death was commemorated on the headstone. From then on, Jack and I were Indian warriors returning to reclaim the land that white men had taken from us. All golfers riding in carts were the cavalry. Those on foot were infantry and the golf clubs they pulled along behind them on wheels were mini cannons. It was us against them. Jack and me against the people in charge of things in this country, the inheritors of power and privilege, the people who were dedicated to keeping everything the way it always had been. After a lifetime of trying to please these people it was pure fun to mess up their golf game. Every morning after we put Erin and Nell on the school bus we went straight to the golf course. There were mornings when we'd find thirty balls or more and return home with our pockets bulging. Some of these balls were handsomely monogrammed with the logos of insurance companies, stock brokerage firms, and resort hotels from as far away as California and Florida. These we saved for a Christmas present for Jack's grandfather.

It was Jack's idea that these monogrammed balls were part of a treasure that had been stolen from us during a battle long ago, and we shook our fists in the air and hollered an Indian war cry whenever we found one. He was a good sport, never complaining of the cold or the thorns or the swamp mud behind the seventh green that on two occasions sucked his boots right off his feet. It wasn't until I found another golf course that paid us a dollar for each ball that he began to protest. I began pushing him too hard and calling him on the carpet when he slacked off. It was just that a hundred balls a week would pay for our groceries, and if we went out every day for four hours and worked steadily, we could find a hundred balls in good enough condition to sell.

"But we were going to give these special balls to Papa," he said disconsolately when I put the monogrammed balls in the Shop & Save bag to sell.

"We need them to make a hundred this week," I said, counting them out.

"That's not fair," he said.

For a few days he stayed at home with his mother, and I went to the golf course alone, where I discovered that his company meant more to me than the economics I'd imposed upon our adventures.

There was a long Indian summer that year, and we spent it on the golf course, where Jack seemed as grateful for our occupation as I was. The more comfortable we grew in our work, the more intricate became our rules of engagement. We could never come out of the woods suddenly, and even if a ball was in plain view we couldn't go after it without first making sure no golfers were in sight. Usually I would cover Jack while he dashed onto the fairway, picked up the ball, and dashed back. Sometimes the balls were still warm, like eggs we'd stolen from a brooding hen. Any golf cart was cause for alarm, but a golf cart with no clubs in back meant the driver was someone from the pro shop prowling the course for trouble. Learning to hide from this authority and from the golfers was not as simple as one might think. It was one thing to conceal ourselves in the bushes but another thing entirely to conceal ourselves and yet still be able to see in all directions. We learned this the hard way one morning when we chased down a ball hit by a golfer off the par three sixth tee. We saw the bad swing and watched the ball land in the woods not more than fifty feet from where we were hiding. When we went to search for it, the golfer and his partners came upon us more quickly than we'd counted on, and when we dove under a fallen cedar tree we lost sight of them. By the time one of the men sat down on the tree three feet from our heads, it was too late to make a run for it.

One morning we found a ball monogrammed with the name of the insurance company that had cut off our automobile policy. I threw it into the ocean. Another time a woman golfer walked into the woods, pulled down her underpants, and peed thirty feet from where we were hiding. I put my hand over Jack's eyes and closed my own.

Eventually we discovered that the golfers were using the fragile sand dunes for a driving range. All along the beach there were signs posted, forbidding the public from walking in the dunes in order to protect the delicate grass that grew there in small green shoots, the land's only defense against erosion. After that the rules of engagement with the enemy changed. I began bringing a golf club along with us and playing the course, stepping out of the woods and hitting my shots as if I had a right to. Instead of hiding from the groundskeepers, we started looking for them. When the guy on the big mower headed down the fairway with his back to us, I would step up and hit a ball over his head then dive into the woods and watch him whip his head around. One morning when four men approached the fourth green, Jack and I shot all ten arrows onto the green. Two of them stuck and stood straight up. "What the hell?" we heard one of the men say. I thought for sure he was going to come into the woods looking for us. Shooting arrows at greens became our favorite act of subversion, but too often the golfers failed to respond and merely threw the arrows off the green as if Indian uprisings were still commonplace in this part of the world. Once, however, a man dressed in clothing so white he looked like a chef kicked our arrows off the green and I heard him say, "I blame some of it on that goddamned rap music."

I told Colleen about this that night in bed. "He was talking about the lack of respect, I guess," I said to her. "That's it, isn't it? The evolution of America has been little more than each generation exposing more fraudulence until no one respects anything anymore and you can be cynical about everything from presidents to doctors to professional athletes."

"I thought your generation started it," she said. "What did you have in mind?"

"So when people talk about the country's loss of innocence, they're really talking about the loss of respect for its institutions."

"You didn't answer me," Colleen said. "Have you thought about what you're teaching Jack on the golf course?"

I stopped long enough to look at her and see that though she knew the answer, she wanted me to say it.

"I don't know," I told her. "It's just nice being out there with him. That's all."

She shook her head and suddenly she was overwhelmed with sadness. "Such a waste of time," she said. "You don't want him to grow up and be one of those people who can never be content with what he has inside him. Someone who makes himself *hate* what these people have here in order to keep from wanting it."

After that I never spoke about our outings. I was pushing my luck and I knew this, but it was so beautiful there, so quiet and peaceful. One day we stayed out on the course until dusk and then walked home the long way past a farmer's stand, where I bought us each a McIntosh apple. I won't forget it. The satisfying sound of us biting into the apples, the sour taste, the purple light on the horizon beyond Stratton Island, three great blue herons heading out to the marsh. "Look around, Jack," I said. "We're really living, buddy!"

And it sure felt like we were. I walked through the woods with Jack, so happy that I began throwing golf balls back out onto the fairway to the golfers who'd hit them into the woods, expecting never to see them again. "Jesus, Paul!" one golfer yelled. "That's one *hell-uv-a* lucky bounce you got."

In late September word came from my friend Robinson that, as he'd predicted at our reunion in Boston, he and Deb had split up. Colleen encouraged me to go visit him, and I took the train down to Florida.

The days there went by quickly, and in no time I was on the train again. All the way home, in Savannah and Richmond, Washington, D.C., Philadelphia, New York, and Boston, the first thing you saw when you pulled into the train station were the homeless people. I thought how sad my grandfathers would be to see these people. Both of those men were laborers who never finished higher than the eighth grade but whose low hourly wage was enough money for them to afford to own a house and to buy a brand-new Ford every three years. Today they would be beggars.

Soon after I got back home I went to the shelter in Portland and took up where Billy had left off, reading the stories of Raymond Carver to the residents who sat against the walls of a square room, most of them with their heads bowed as if they were in church. My first night there a short, pie-faced man with a black knit ski hat pulled down over his ears and an ugly gash across the bridge of his nose stood up suddenly in the middle of one story and recited Kipling's poem "If" by heart. The next night a gangly fellow with thick, black-rimmed glasses and wild eyes stood up and walked toward me with his right hand out. When I reached out to shake it, he pulled his hand away and leaned up against me. He put his lips to my ear and whispered, "Let me be the first person here NOT to shake your hand, and not to give a SHIT what you have to say."

A week or so later I found out from the woman in charge that this man had a wife and three small children in South Portland whom he had abandoned when his wife was diagnosed with terminal cancer. They had had a decent life; he was a stevedore and had once made good money. They had a three-year-old son and a five-year-old daughter when she went into the hospital to deliver a new baby. While she was there lumps were discovered in her breasts.

By the time she came home with her new baby daughter she knew that the cancer had already spread into her lymph nodes and she was probably going to die. When her husband fell into a paralyzing depression and could no longer work, they moved into her mother's house. He began walking the streets all night long. And then, one morning he stopped coming home.

Their story was the saddest story I'd ever heard. I became obsessed with them. Eventually the woman who ran the shelter told me that the father had hit bottom when he was unable to take his family to Disney World. It was the only thing his wife asked for, a family trip to Disney World before she no longer had the strength for such a journey.

One September afternoon when it felt cold enough to snow I walked up Temple Street in South Portland with my two oldest daughters to where the mother was living. There were dark clouds overhead and there was a threatening orange light on the horizon.

"I'm cold," Nell said, taking my hand.

I wasn't going to go up to the door, I knew that. I guess I just wanted to see the house and to know how they were living there. We stood at the corner at first and then we walked down the sidewalk to the one-story ranch house covered in white vinyl siding. It was kept as neat as a ship. The garage door was up and there was a picnic table sitting there and you could see that the garage had been converted to a dining room. We watched as a gray-haired woman began setting the table. There was a red wagon, an old model with the wooden sides like the one my grandfather used to pull me and my twin brother in when we moved into his house after my mother died. The house was quiet. We went up the street a bit farther so we could see into the backyard. The grass was newly cut and the clothesline was full of children's clothing, some things no bigger than a doll's. Then it began to rain. Lightly, just a shower. But at the moment it started, almost with the very first drops, she came out the back door. It was as if she'd been sitting at the window, keeping watch over her children's clothes. She looked strong, like so many Maine women are. Broad shoulders. Thick hips. But her hair was too black, with curls too symmetrical to be real, and when she walked down the steps from the porch she held on to both railings. I saw her pain when she reached up for the clothesline. It was a motion she made slowly and deliberately. What she did was take hold of the clothesline and slowly pull it down, pulling the slack out of the rope while she lifted her arm over it and held it against her ribs. This way she took the laundry down without having to raise her arms again. She walked slowly along the lawn, with the clothesline under her arm, taking off the pins and just letting everything drop into a basket she pushed along the ground with one foot.

"Is that her?" Erin asked me.

"Daddy, hold my hand tighter," Nell whispered.

I looked down at her and saw her lift her eyes to me. We only stayed a little while. Then we went to the rectory of the church where I'd learned this woman worshiped. I had emptied our checking account that afternoon and had seventeen hundred dollars in cash in an envelope. At first I had been cynical about it. Who in their right mind would choose to spend their final days in a theme park? And what kind of man would allow his life to blow up just because he couldn't take his family there? But once I stopped judging them, I wanted to help. At the rectory I explained to the priest what the money was for, and when I put it in his hand he smiled at me and then at the girls.

I hadn't said anything about this to Colleen because I was afraid that even the slightest objection from her would make me stop and think about what I was going to do. All I wanted was a clean break from the past sixteen months, when the money that I had counted and coveted and budgeted would finally be gone. I had dreamed about this money. I had spent whole days thinking about what it might get for us and how I could use it wisely. I had bought some time with it, and then used the time foolishly.

189

I admit that there was more to it than all of this. It was a play against fate, and even as the priest opened his desk drawer and slid the money inside, I was hoping that fate or God would look upon me with favor now and would turn my luck so that I could find a way back to my old life.

"Lovely," the priest said. "May God go with you."

The next morning I told Colleen what I had done. She stood at the kitchen sink, washing dishes, her back to me as I explained that the next check we wrote would bounce. "We're broke," I said. "All the money is gone." She didn't say anything, she just kept washing dishes. Finally I told her I was going to go look for work.

I walked to the golf course, to the cinder block shed off the seventh tee, where I asked the greenskeeper for a job.

13

He was just a taciturn, middle-aged guy in tan work pants and a Boston Celtics jacket who kept the radio in the garage tuned to an AM talk show that made fun of blacks, environmentalists, women in general, and Hillary Clinton, specifically, all day long. He asked me if I felt comfortable around machinery. Typewriters, I was thinking. Copy machines. "Sure," I told him. That was part of the job; the other part was running trespassers off the course. "Gee," I said innocently, "this time of year I wouldn't think you'd have much of a problem." One of the other workers said, "We get kids from town out here sometimes. Somebody shot a bow and arrow at a couple of golfers."

"Really?"

"Pay is seven bucks an hour," the boss said.

*　　*　　*

We started at sunrise and I got up at four the next morning, afraid that I might oversleep. "Where are you going?" Colleen asked when I bumped into the bedroom door. I walked back to the bed, leaned over, and kissed her. "Work," I said. And I was immediately filled with a sense of well-being that stayed with me while I sat in the kitchen, drinking coffee and writing letters to each of the kids in their journals. I wrote merrily, waiting for the sun to come up. I hadn't written in Jack's book since the day after I was fired.

The sense of well-being would have been difficult to describe at the time. It wasn't so much a personal thing as it was a large, all-encompassing sense that some order and clarity had fallen across the world. I think this was the time when the Hutu and Tutsi tribes of Rwanda were engaged in mind-boggling slaughter. I could never keep straight from one hour to the next which tribe was guilty of the killing, but nevertheless my mind tried desperately to reconcile this human tragedy with the new sense of equanimity that ran through me and left me feeling at times intoxicated.

My first few days at work I rode around with Cal on a Cushman golf cart equipped with a bed in back where we carried shovels and buckets of high-potency grass seed. We stopped the cart wherever there were divots in the fairways, hopped out, sprinkled some grass seed, and drove off. Cal was seventy-five years old, he'd been working at the golf course for fifteen years since retiring from a shipbuilding plant in southern Maine, and he was still under the spell of the beauty of the place. He would stop the cart to point out a flock of geese overhead, and we never drove by a sand trap without him slowing down so he could check for animal tracks. Years earlier he had found the tracks of what he was sure was a bobcat, and this had thrilled him so much that every day he expected to see them again. Our first week together he shared with me his secret places where you could stop and have a wonderful view and a cigarette without the boss finding you. "When you get to be my age," he told me, "you mellow out and just enjoy life. I don't ever kick anybody off this golf course. Hell, it's a private park for the rich buggers, and I figure everybody should get to enjoy it. There's a guy and his little boy who come out here practically every day. They have a good time, I think."

Joe, a sweet guy in his early twenties with a wife and a newborn first baby, taught me how to drive the Greensmaster 3000, a complex mower that trimmed the greens. This job had been Edgar's, who was a twenty-five-year-old veteran of the Gulf War, which he referred to disdainfully as the "*Golf* War," and he still spoke proudly of how straight his lines had always been until he lost his steadiness to the war and was demoted.

The three of them, Cal, Joe, and Edgar, came to represent to me the past, present, and future of America. Cal loved America and spoke solemnly about her beauty and greatness. He grew up on a farm in Maine and had brushed his teeth every morning of his life in his father's farmhouse until he enlisted in the army at age eighteen. He was in combat in the Philippines for three years and participated in some of the bloodiest contests of World War II, yet when he spoke of those days it was always with a smile. "I remember how close you got to your buddies," he told me. "And how you looked forward to little things like dry socks and the taste of coffee." After working thirty years in the shipyard and putting his kids through college Cal bought a motorcycle, and with his wife on back he drove it across America, deciding along the way that he lived in the most beautiful country on earth.

Unlike Cal, who dressed every day in neatly pressed khakis top and bottom and a short-waisted jacket like the Eisenhower jackets of his war, Joe came to work with his shirttails out, his hair uncombed, and his head spinning from the morning race to get his newborn to the day care center and his wife to the job that she had to work six days a week in order for them to pay their rent and the payments on their new minivan, which Joe suspected would begin to fall apart as soon as the warranty expired. What he looked forward to and spoke of with the wistfulness of a man twice his age was the time to spend with his wife and child, and less hurried days.

Edgar, married and father of a two-year-old, had already concluded that no matter how hard he worked he was never going to get anywhere.

At first when I walked by our mailbox on my way home from the golf course every afternoon I didn't bother checking for job letters. It just felt so good to be back in the working world that I didn't want to do anything that might break the spell or the new rhythm of my working days. Because we started so early each morning, I got home in time to lie on the couch with Jack and watch *Dennis the Menace, Flipper,* and *Gilligan's Island* back to back without a serious thought in my head. I took whatever was in front of me — a few tender minutes with a child in my lap, a plate of food, a glass of beer, a sunrise, the chance to feel my wife's skin against mine, a fresh, honey-dipped donut — and didn't think beyond it.

And for a while this was enough. I woke happily at four every morning, hit the floor for fifty push-ups and a hundred sit-ups, drank an enormous mug of French vanilla or hazelnut-flavored coffee, ate five donuts, and wrote in the kids' journals while sitting in front of the window where the sun rose over the ocean. It always gave me a rush of pleasure and adrenaline when morning light began to seep through the darkness and I could write, "Daddy has to go off to work now."

But after a few weeks I rode around on the golf cart repairing the fairways, or on the Greensmaster 3000 mowing the greens, and the only thing that could quiet the anger in my soul were the lyrics of Bruce Springsteen, lyrics of the dispossessed and the humiliated played at a deafening volume in my headphones. Part of the trouble was that with the exception of the few days it took to learn to operate each new piece of machinery, every eight-hour shift was filled with murderous monotony. I started smoking heavily just to help pass the time. And for the first time in my life I began drinking more than one beer in the evening in order to dull the dread that accompanied each thought about returning to work the next morning.

Boredom and the mindless repetition were part of it, but mainly what killed the job for me was the reality that working for seven dollars an hour meant that at the end of each week I brought home just about half of what we needed to keep from falling even farther behind. Once I figured this out, I grew angrier and angrier. There was an evening when I was making spaghetti for dinner and I couldn't find whatever the thing is called that you use to drain the pasta.

"A colander," Colleen said.

"Well, why don't we have one?"

"I just haven't wanted to spend the money."

"Well, for God's sake, how much can one of them cost?"

"We don't have *any* extra money."

God damn it! I thought. I threw open the window above the sink, took out the screen, and strained the noodles through it.

*   *   *

Colleen applied for food stamps on her own, and when they arrived she put them in the back of a desk drawer. She found me counting them one night and she said, "I'll go do the shopping from now on. You don't have to do it."

I didn't want her to have to be the one who stood at the cash register counting them out for the cashier, but I let her go. She took Erin with her and when they got back, Erin gave me a scornful glance as she passed me on the couch. "What?" I called to her.

She stopped and turned to face me. "You made us use those stupid tickets," she yelled. Then she started to cry and ran off to her room.

Nell came into the kitchen later while Colleen and I were putting the groceries away. She wanted to know what was wrong with her sister.

"Nothing," I said. "She's just spoiled." Colleen didn't say anything. Then I noticed that all the groceries were the most practical things, potatoes, eggs, flour, bread. And all of it was the cheap store brand.

"We need to get some real food in this house," I said. "We should stock the kitchen and throw a party or something. How about a neighborhood party?"

"No one else lives here," Nell pointed out sweetly.

"You're right," I said to her, "but come on, you'll go shopping with me, won't you?"

We walked up and down the aisles together. "Just one indulgence," I said to my daughter when we decided on shrimp.

As we stood in line in the checkout aisle a young man in a beautiful camel's hair overcoat came up behind us. The woman on his arm was wearing a black cocktail dress slit up one thigh. As soon as I started to pay for the shrimp with food stamps I heard the man groan. I was already nervous about the transaction, afraid the cashier might ask me for some kind of identification that I didn't have. I don't know what the man said to the woman, but when she sighed, I told myself to hit him first and then say whatever came to mind. Instead I turned and faced him. "Nell," I said, "you know why this man is groaning? If we were buying boxes of macaroni and cheese with our food stamps it would be all right with him, but we're buying shrimp, and he's groaning about it because that's the kind of food he eats." He turned and walked toward the next aisle. The woman looked back at me with disgust.

The rest of the day I felt like I was right back in the early days after we had left Colgate. The anger left the same taste in my mouth. I kept drifting back to the supermarket, dreaming up these clever things I should have said to the woman to put her in her place. My head was still pounding when I put the kids to bed that night.

"Who's moving in tonight, Daddy?" Nell asked. "Which cottage?"

"It's my turn to pick!" Jack hollered.

"I think it's Erin's turn," I said.

Erin rolled over and faced the wall. "Jack can have my turn," she said disconsolately.

"Yippee!" he cheered.

I told him to thank his sister. I sat down on Erin's bed to tell the nightly installment of my invented bedtime story about Portland's homeless people taking up residence as our winter neighbors in the empty cottages at Prouts Neck. Each night one of the kids would pick a cottage, and then I'd have to make up the rest. The stories always ended with me explaining why the person had wound up without a home of his own.

Tonight Jack chose the cottage at the end of our lane and I

told the tale of Henrietta Wapshot, who had danced on Broadway as a young girl with her identical twin brother, Wilhelm. At age fifteen she accepted a full scholarship to the Juilliard School of Music, and all through her twenties she was a ballerina with the Boston Ballet Company.

"Was she pretty?" Nell asked.

"Extraordinary."

"Like Mommy?" Jack asked.

"Very much like Mommy," I said.

I saw Cara start to scratch her nose, the last thing she did at the end of her busy, busy days before her elevator finally dropped into the basement with a sigh and she closed her eyes for the night.

I lay down next to Erin and went on telling the story. "Henrietta Wapshot is moving in tonight. She has long silver hair and green eyes. She's bringing all her precious possessions in a brown suitcase with the handle missing. In the morning if you look in the window next to the stone chimney, you'll see it standing on the floor."

"Why did she get to be homeless?" Erin asked suddenly.

"I'm not there yet, sweetie," I said. "It looks like a suitcase, but it's actually a small record player."

"She plays music when she practices her ballet!" Nell proclaimed proudly.

"Exactly. She has only one record, and if you listen carefully you'll hear it every time you walk by the cottage."

"How come she doesn't have a house?" Jack asked.

"Well, it's very simple," I said. "One night in 1947 she was walking home from the ballet, where she had performed Snow White. A crowd of people had gathered at one street corner, and when she approached she saw smoke coming from an upstairs window and a young boy perched on the windowsill, afraid to jump to safety. Everyone was just standing there, watching, so Henrietta ran closer and yelled to the boy to jump into her coat, which she held out in front of her like a net. 'It's all right,' she yelled to the boy. 'Jump!' He did, but he had eaten a lot of ice cream and cake in his life and he was very heavy—"

"Like Mr. Big Butt on the golf course?" Jack asked eagerly.

"Well, maybe not that fat, but he was too heavy nonetheless, and when Henrietta caught him and saved him she injured her back and could never dance again, so she had no means of earning money."

"Why didn't she find a job doing something else?" Nell asked.

"She tried. She worked lots of jobs, but she always had to quit because they made her too sad. She was a dancer, and that was all she was."

"What about her brother?" Nell asked.

"He had his own problems. He didn't have time to help her."

When I kissed Jack goodnight I whispered into his ear, "Always take care of your sisters, Bunky."

"I will," he said. I was heading out of the room when Erin said, "So she had to use those food tickets then?"

I couldn't believe that she was still angry about this, and I was trying to think of what to say to her when Colleen spoke from the doorway. "Yes," she said. "She used them and she held her head up anyway because she was doing the best that she could and she respected herself."

When we were alone in front of the fire I thanked her. "Erin should have been born to a father who could slip her a credit card and send her off to a gift shop," I said.

"What about you?" Colleen asked me suddenly. "What do you want do do? You can do whatever you want to do."

"Do you really believe that?" I asked her.

She spoke about her two grandfathers, who had come to this country with barely any education and nothing in their pockets. One made himself into a successful farmer, the other built a happy life as the manager of a grocery store.

"That was a long time ago," I told her.

"So?"

"Things are harder today."

"Do you really think they are? How can they be harder than what they faced?" she said. "I think you look down on people who just do regular jobs so they can pay their way. I don't. I've never thought one person was better than another person because of the job he does, but I think you do. I think you always have."

14

One morning I was riding down the eighteenth fairway with the boss beside me in the Cushman golf truck, headed for the practice tee, where we were in the middle of a big excavation project to improve drainage. Cal was always the first one to work, but I hadn't seen him this morning and I asked where he was. "Called in sick," the boss said with a sneer. "Shit, I feel sick every fuckin' morning of my life, but I get to work."

It was Cal's extreme loyalty to this job and to this man that made me so angry. Cal was seventy-five years old, he was the first one in line for every tough job that had to be done on the golf course, and this man was deriding him behind his back. The rest of the day I was burning up over this. I shoveled dirt for seven hours and before I left for home I quit. I lied to the guy and said that I had to go out of town.

Colleen's dad was at the cottage when I got home and I lied to him too. "My last day at the golf course," I said to him casually. "Laid off." It was an easy lie and Colleen believed it as well.

I expected to get up the next morning and go out looking for another job, but through the night I lay awake going over this litany in my head — *I was a great teacher. I don't deserve this kind of crap. I gave my money away to a dying mother. I brought a sick student into my house. I deserve better than this!* I could feel it starting all over again, the anger and the self-rightousness filling my sails.

Almost the next day the first rejection from my latest round of applications arrived. Then three more that knocked me back into bed for two weeks while the autumn leaves blew down.

Winter came on quickly. One morning I woke and saw my breath. Downstairs the cottage was freezing, so I walked to the beach and filled a canvas bag with driftwood for a fire. This became my first light routine each day. I would build a roaring fire in the living room so that when the kids got up there was one warm room where they could get dressed for school and eat their breakfast.

We were down to our last fifty dollars the morning when, out on my driftwood walk, I saw what I thought at first was a mirage, the kind where sunlight shimmers above the mudflats like ribbons of heat off a highway. It looked like ladders, hundreds and hundreds of wooden ladders standing on the ledges half a mile away. I kept walking until I got close enough to see clearly the enormous wood frame of a structure that looked much too large to be a house. I stared at it for a while then went back home.

I was reading the help wanted pages when Colleen came into the kitchen carrying Cara, who was crying at the top of her lungs. "I slammed the door on her finger, poor thing," I heard Colleen say sorrowfully as she set Cara down on the counter and took off her little blue mitten. Then I heard her scream. "Her finger came off! The top of her finger came off! Call John Bradford and tell him to help us!"

While I was on the telephone dialing 911 and thinking dismally that nothing like this had ever happened when I had health insurance, Colleen disappeared with Cara.

A marvelous hand surgeon operated on her and saved her finger. It was more than just my desire to pay him what he deserved that carried me back to the house to ask for a job. It was the memory of me just standing there in the kitchen, standing inside my fears and taking all that time to feel sorry for myself while Colleen wrapped Cara's hand in a dish towel, zipped her inside her down coat, and, afraid that the ambulance would not find them, ran down the lane and out the main road in the direction of the hospital seven miles away.

I walked back to the house the next morning, very early, I guess to show whoever was in charge that he could count on me not to be late for work. A cold, hard wind was kicking up big waves in the cove. I walked the quarter mile to the end of the beach, then climbed the rocks to a narrow path that bordered the promontory where the handsome summer cottages stood looking out to sea. This was Colleen's favorite part of Prouts Neck. She called the path the cliff walk, and she went there often to gather bittersweet and driftwood. I stopped on the footbridge that crossed a gorge. From this close the house looked big enough to be a hotel. The wood frame rose three stories from the foundation, each story twelve or fourteen feet high. I guessed the structure to be maybe a hundred feet by forty feet, with a roofline that was fifty feet from the ground. The bottom ten feet of concrete basement wall was being overlaid with beautiful granite stones. I saw three men working on one part of the wall. The first man stared down at a pile of stones, then picked up one and passed it slowly to a second man, who walked the stone to a third man, who was down on his knees at the foundation wall waiting to set it in place. I was thinking that surely they knew anything built this close to the Atlantic Ocean would eventually be washed out to sea.

There were four carpenters nailing sheets of plywood to the wooden frame. They moved along quickly through the studs, climbing and descending like acrobats, leather tool pouches belted around their waist, trailing long hoses behind them that supplied the air for their pneumatic hammers that went off like gunshots in the stillness. I watched a man hoist a sheet of plywood into place with one arm while he held on to the frame with the other. I was looking at them the way you watch the other team working out before a game, measuring yourself against them.

Before I walked out into view, I took off my woolen hat and scarf and stuffed them in my coat pockets so that I would come across as a guy who wasn't bothered by the weather. But by the time I picked my way through the marsh thickets I was cold to the center of my bones and I wished I hadn't come at all.

Larry, the contractor, had to finish cutting out a section of plywood for a window with a long-toothed vibrating saw that made his shoulders shake like a machine gunner. He dropped the saw with disdain when he was done and swung down through the frame, jumping the final four feet. He had the grin of a schoolboy who had just pulled one over on his headmaster. He looked happy and fit enough to build the place by himself, but as it turned out, I'd chosen a perfect day to hit him up for work. You could feel winter bearing down hard, and we stood talking in the midst of an equation that even his ferocious energy couldn't change: there was a mountain of a house left to build, and only a stretch of blistering cold days left in which to build it.

It would be outside work, all winter. There was the rest of the plywood sheathing, then the whole structure had to be wrapped, then the windows and doors, roof, trim, decks, and porches. He went through it all dispassionately. "Maybe a month and a half of shingling alone," he said. "Have you put on cedar shingles before?"

I lied to him for the first time. "It's a big house," I said, looking up to the roof.

"It's a dream," he said. He told me it was almost fourteen thousand square feet and it might end up costing a million five to finish. He'd built a couple of ranch houses before — dollhouses compared to this. "It's the same thing, though," he said. "You build one house, there's no mystery to the next one."

I liked him instantly and felt bad that I was going to have to hide from him the crushed disc in my back and everything that I didn't know about carpentry. It went through my mind how I would end up dropping something like an expensive window or cutting a pile of boards a half inch too short. I looked up again and wondered how in God's name you could work on the steep pitches of the roof without falling off when it was covered with snow and ice.

He told me I could start as soon as I wanted. "We work ten-hour days, and I'll pay you fifteen dollars an hour," he said.

"I'll start tomorrow morning," I said.

"Just bring your carpenter's belt," he said as he jumped back onto the framed wall and began climbing. He was above my head when he called out, "You have a carpenter's belt?"

I lied to him again.

I walked down Winslow Homer Lane, going over the numbers in my head. *Fifteen bucks an hour times ten hours a day times five days a week. Plenty. Plenty.* By the time I reached the electronic gate and ducked under its arm I was thinking I would take Colleen out for dinner, maybe buy her a new dress.

Later that day I took all four kids with me to Wal-Mart to buy a carpenter's belt. I tried it on for them and showed them the leather pockets for a tape measure and knife, the pouches for nails, and the clip that would hold my hammer. We gave Cara a ride on the mechanical horse. I watched Erin's surprise when I handed her some quarters for the gum ball machine; for months I had tried hard to convince her that we weren't poor, just broke, and now I wanted her to see me spend some money. As soon as we got home I went into the kitchen and took the food stamps from the cupboard, where we kept them in a glass jar. That night I threw them into the fire while Erin was watching. She asked me, "Who bought those tickets for us anyway?" I told her that people who had jobs bought them. She wanted to know why. "Because they're earning money," I said, "and it's only fair that they should help people who aren't earning money." I looked at her as she tried to figure this out. I could almost see her recounting this scene for her investment banker husband fifteen years down the road who chuckles along with her and says, *"Baby, no wonder you guys were always so poor. Your old man was a hopeless romantic."* It was for him, the future husband, that I continued on awhile longer, trying to impress upon my daughter that the notion of a lucky person helping an unlucky person was the only thing that held civilization together.

"Well," she said softly, "I don't think that we should use them again."

"All right," I said, "but look at it this way. If your sister, Nell, was hungry and she couldn't buy food because she didn't have enough money, would you buy food for her?"

She rolled her eyes and said, "Well, you should just keep having a job, that's all."

At six in the morning I made a thermos of tea and two peanut butter and jelly sandwiches, then put on all the warm clothes I had, undershirt, long johns top and bottom, two pairs of wool socks, turtleneck, cotton shirt buttoned at the neck, jeans, flannel shirt, wool sweater. It took me about as long to dress as it had to put on my goalie equipment when I played ice hockey. Over the top I wore the heavy quilted greatcoat that my father-in-law had worn to work the docks in South Portland. The only gloves I could find that were thin enough to grip a hammer and nails and still looked fairly warm were bright yellow cotton ones for $2.29 in a bin by the ice-cream freezer at Shop & Save.

At six-thirty I left the house with the empty carpenter's belt hanging from my waist. It was colder outside than it had been the day before. The sand along the shore was frozen as hard as cement. I wore the only boots I owned, a pair of Wellingtons, and I could feel my toes going numb by the time I walked the beach and reached the main road.

From the top of the promontory, Ram Island, six miles north, was swimming in plum-colored light. Beyond the shipping lanes a small parade of fishing boats worked their way farther out to sea.

I stepped inside the house through an opening in the studs where a chimney was going up. It was like standing inside the ruins of some great cathedral with vaulted ceilings and high walls and long wide floors. The charging waves and the jagged black rocks pressing up to the unfinished walls and the freezing sky that was falling through the open roof all gave the impression that a struggle was taking place. The house itself was at the stage where it looked just as much like a house that was being torn down as one that was being built.

Larry arrived just as I finished rubbing my new carpenter's belt in sawdust to try to make it look old. He got out of his red Ford truck with a pot of coffee in one hand and a canvas attaché in the other. Under one arm he had a roll of blueprints. He yelled good morning, asked me if I didn't own any better boots, and gestured with the coffeepot to follow him.

"I've wanted to get this beam up," he said, setting everything down on the plywood floor. I took a look at it. Three hundred pounds. Colleen's mom, a nurse, had lectured me about stretching exercises since I had crushed a disc in my back, but I was of the unenlightened old school of athletes who believed that stretching was for the self-righteous joggers who crept along the side of the road in hundred-dollar running shoes or the bicyclists dressed up like court jesters.

I looked hard at the beam. Larry explained where it had to go and how we were going to lift it over our heads together, one end at a time, and it was going to be a piece of cake. He took the time to go over his plan again, then paused and eyed the beam with relish. When we were getting into place he told me about a children's book he read to his girls every night. "It's all about these lumberjacks in the Maine woods, you know?" We stood side by side, bent down together, and on the count of three raised the beam, first to our waist, then to our shoulders. "*Push!* How they used to move logs down the rivers, and how they'd strip them. It's great." Slowly we climbed the ladder with the beam. "*Easy, easy.* Every night, I say , 'Okay, what book do you want me to read to you tonight, girls?' And before they can answer, I pull out the lumberjack book — 'How about this one, girls?' *Okay, on the count of three then. You ready? One, two, three!"* We got the end just above the top of the wall, where it was going to be nailed into place to hold the floor above it. "Drive a couple spikes in it before it kills us," Larry groaned. He was above me one step on the ladder with his shoulder and his head pressed against the beam. I couldn't help him. Finally he looked at me. *"You got nails?"* he hollered.

"I didn't bring any tools," I said. He gave me a curious look and then saw my empty carpenter's belt. "I thought you just wanted me to bring my belt," I said.

I knew at once what had happened. When he had told me I didn't need to bring tools to this job he meant power tools, and when I'd lied to him that I had a carpenter's belt he assumed I didn't mean an empty one that was as useless as a prop I'd picked up on my way from central casting. It was the sort of moment you hope you can redeem yourself from and joke about someday.

I was issued a tape measure, hammer, two chisels, a knife, and a pencil. I filled the leather pouches with nails and wore the belt low on one hip like a gunslinger's holster the way the rest of the crew wore theirs. At the end of the day, rather than hang it up, I kept mine on under my overcoat and walked home. Everyone was having supper when I came into the kitchen, and I saw their eyes open wide when I dropped my coat on a chair and unhitched the belt as casually as if I'd been wearing it my whole working life.

I learned the history of the house on my first dump run when I told the men who were waiting in line, smoking cigarettes and leaning against their pickups, that I was working at Prouts Neck. One of the guys, a roofer with a face as hard as a hatchet, said he'd showed up there one day during the summer to ask about work, but there wasn't anyone around. He'd found out from a couple of carpenters one morning at the donut shop on Route 1 that the house had caused trouble among the summer people right from the beginning when a young lawyer bought the piece of land that everyone at Prouts Neck believed to be wetlands that could not be developed. Most of the house would have been finished long before now if the community of Prouts Neck hadn't formed a committee to shut down construction. Throughout the summer the buyer walked a narrow line, trying to get his house built without permanently pissing off the people who would become his seasonal neighbors.

The guys at the dump laughed about this. One of them, a gray-haired painter in a Red Sox cap, said he had done some work on one of the Prouts Neck houses one spring and the owner, rather than reveal to him the combination on the electronic gate, met him at the gate each morning at six o'clock. "I knew the combination was fourteen-ninety-two," he said disdainfully, "but I didn't mind getting the guy out of bed. Fourteen-ninety-two," he said, shaking his head. "As if they discovered the damned place."

I told him that the new combination was 6-6-4-4.

"D day," he said at once, shaking his head again.

It hadn't dawned on me.

For three days I worked with Billy, wrapping the back end of the house with some polyester material that has replaced the more modest tar paper and that felt to me exactly like a pair of bell bottom pants I once owned. The name of the product, TyPAR, was stamped in huge letters every couple feet so that a house under construction, before the outer walls are covered, is a giant billboard advertisement for the manufacturer. A full roll weighed fifty pounds, and Billy and I worked on two ladders passing the

210

roll back and forth and leapfrogging one another as we went along tacking it to the plywood with heavy-duty staplers that made a thunking sound that Billy imitated the whole time we worked, rather than talk to me. He'd been introduced to me as Larry's partner, and I took his silence to mean he wasn't sure I was worth the fifteen dollars an hour that Larry had offered to pay me. I had heard from a guy at the dump that Billy had grown up summering down the shore near Kennebunk, which was how he met and married President Bush's daughter.

Billy coached a high school ice hockey team and had to leave work on Friday afternoon for practice. Before he climbed down from his ladder he told me to nail the last sheet of plywood in place on the east wall before I finished up. *Myself?* I thought as he walked away. I tried three times to climb the ladder with the four-by-eight sheet of plywood but my arms went numb before I reached the top and I had to drop the thing and start again. It took me so long that when I finally made it up the ladder and onto the scaffolding, everyone else had gone home and it was nearly dark. Forty feet below me the waves were bashing the granite ledges and throwing a salt spray against the house that had iced the plank of wood beneath my feet. The instant I raised the plywood off the plank to set it in place the wind caught one corner of it and spun me around. I grabbed an iron bar of the scaffold with my left hand and held on. I was thinking, *How in God's name would Billy or any other real carpenter have done this?* It was a strange moment. The blood ran out of my arms and there was a pain in my back like a cold spark. I heard the waves crashing on the rocks and I felt the wind wash over me and a lightness fill my lungs. For more than a year I'd had the sensation that I was falling backward, and now I felt like I had arrived where I was supposed to be. I thought, *All I have to do is lean back slightly onto my heels and let the wind take hold of me and the sheet of plywood and I'll rise up into the winter sky, set free from everything.* There was that. And there was the screened-in sleeping porch on the back of the house where my family was now. I could just make it out down the shore. I began thinking about how nice it would be on summer nights to have a screened-in porch like that to sleep out on with Colleen and the kids. I built that porch in my mind and then built it again until I had the sheet of plywood nailed in place and was climbing down the scaffolding.

There were six of us working on the crew, but because the house was so large that over the course of any given day we might not see one another, Larry insisted that we all take our fifteen-minute coffee break and our half-hour lunch together whenever possible. He usually made the coffee, and personally gave the Rebel yell — "Coffeeeeeee!" — that could be heard above the howling power tools and the growling bulldozers and backhoes. We were his crew and he wanted us to appreciate one another. Once I walked right by a man in my haste to get back to a second-story deck where I had been tearing down staging. Larry saw this and he climbed down from the third story to set me straight. "You can't just walk by people," he said. "It's going to be a long winter."

We took our breaks in the basement, in a makeshift room the carpenters had built, consisting of studded walls and a ceiling stuffed with yellow fiberglass insulation and covered with clear plastic. Two four-foot lengths of electric baseboard heat had been hooked up along the cement floor, as well as a single light bulb that swung from the center of the ceiling. The room was roughly the size of an ordinary kitchen and accommodated the six of us, plus a large, hastily made table for tools and a small desk in one corner where there was a telephone, answering machine, and a stack of blueprints. The doorway was rigged with another sheet of clear plastic, weighted at the bottom by a stick of wood. We stripped off our clothing the second we entered the room so that we wouldn't sweat and so we'd feel the warmth when we went back out. Sometimes we sat there as silent as monks, heads bowed, each one of us too cold and numb to speak. In the early days, when my body was trying to get used to the cold, I sat there forcing myself to stay alert by trying to say just under my breath the names of the forty-seven colleges I still hadn't heard from but might hear from when I got home after work.

I thought of the place as a locker room, the kind of male sanctuary where we would have been less surprised to hear gunfire than a female voice. In this room I got to know them, listening carefully while they consulted one another with whatever problem they faced on the job, drawing pencil diagrams on the cement floor to explain themselves, or gathering around the blueprints. These few minutes in the locker room were the only downtime in the crew's ten-hour workday, but each of them seemed to know intuitively how enormous the job was, and how no time could be wasted if it was going to be completed on schedule.

Rob was twenty-five, a strong and talented carpenter who had the rugged good looks of a ski bum. He ate gourmet food that his mother-in-law cooked, bringing it to work in Tupperware containers that he propped against the baseboard heaters with scraps of wood so it would be warm by noon. He had spent time playing golf in Ireland and spoke tenderly of long-ago hunting and fishing trips with his father. He believed firmly that Americans had to start taking responsibility for their lives, and paydays always put him in bad spirits from the moment he opened his check and saw how much he had lost to taxes.

Mark was a tall, big-shouldered bear of a man, also in his

twenties. He had traveled the country and looked into college before getting married and teaching himself how to build things. Patient and soft-spoken, he had the sweet disposition of a guy who would volunteer to be Santa Claus at the Christmas party. His specialty was fine finish work, kitchen cabinets, and furniture, and he had an eye so true and accurate that we all relied upon it as we did our levels and tape measures.

Luke, by the time he turned thirty, had used his liberal arts education from Kenyon College to learn all there was to know about working with steel, wood, concrete, electricity, pumps, engines, explosives, and heavy construction equipment, and his knowledge had earned him the only title in the crew, that of project manager. The desk in the locker room belonged to him, and he spent his days there, in warmth that the rest of us could only dream about, reading about new construction materials and techniques, ordering materials and riding herd over the bids that were coming in from subcontractors. He had movie star good looks and a stunning wardrobe that helped define the dividing line between management and labor.

Guy, a shy French Canadian in his early fifties, drove an ancient, punched-in, pale blue van that was crammed with everything necessary for a man to work and live, including the sardines he brought for lunch. He was an itinerant carpenter with pale, thoughtful eyes, and such an astonishing knowledge of ways to undo mistakes that he was consulted like a country doctor.

Billy was in his late thirties, sad eyed, taciturn, and as strong as an ox. He had played college hockey with Boston University in that school's glory days in the late 1970s and then was invited to the Olympic tryout in Colorado, where the team that went on to steal the gold medal from the Russians was assembled.

Larry had the heart of a sled dog, and he outworked everyone, and we all marveled at him. He was a thirty-four-year-old man who wasn't fully happy unless he was sweaty and covered with dirt, and he gave the impression that he would have been perfectly willing to finish his coffee and then go perform open-heart surgery if someone just handed him the right tools. A graduate of Wake Forest, he only lost his patience and his affection for the project when he was forced to do paperwork, and nothing would have pleased him more than to have been born before electricity, when every task would have been harder.

I was the rookie and in the locker room I took some ribbing for being a professor. I came in for lunch once after painting all morning. "What have you been painting?" Mark asked.

"Garage doors," I said.

"Did you get any on the doors?" he said.

Mostly they teased me about my boots. Riding boots they called them. "Where'd you leave your horse today, Professor? . . . I bet you need a good pair of high boots like that to teach in."

My boots were the first thing Cal noticed when he stopped by one day to say hello. "Those were all right for the golf course, but you won't survive the winter in boots like that," he said. I was carrying lumber and I dragged out the job so we could talk. He told me he was going to the doctor in the morning because he was having trouble pissing. "You get old, things stop working," he said with a smile. He knew Larry and believed him to be one of the people who was going to save America. "He believes in the working man," he told me. "He could pay you guys half of what he does and he'd put all that extra money in his pocket when he walks away from this place next summer. It's a matter of greed. We need more people like him who do the right thing just because it's right, even if it costs him some money."

One day in the locker room Luke said to me, "Once you start

shingling this place we'll have to scrape the ice off you before you come in for coffee."

Billy heard this and began imitating the sound of nailing on shingles—"Tink-tink. Tink-tink." Someone else said, "Hope you find some better boots." I laughed along with them and didn't dare tell them how I was looking forward to that job. After three weeks I had pretty much revealed all my inadequacies, and most days now I spent sweeping scrap lumber into piles, loading the piles into trash cans, lugging the trash cans to Larry's truck, and then driving to the dump. No matter how many times Larry told me how good a job I was doing, and how important it was to keep the job site clean because it reflected on the company, I knew I was a fifteen-dollar-an-hour trash man who occasionally got to carry lumber or take nails out of boards, and though I was just as cold as anyone else and my clothes were just as dirty, when I came into the locker room for coffee break I didn't feel like I'd earned it. I always looked at Billy and figured he wasn't speaking to me because he was *building a house* and he hadn't figured out yet what the hell I was doing. It was like standing outside reading a book in a freezing cold wind, on a busy street with traffic roaring by, reading page after page and trying to grab hold of the meaning of the pages amid the noise and the cold, but the paragraphs just turn into more paragraphs and no story ever begins. I kept looking for the narrative in my work, something that was moving forward and that would add up to a house. Instead I worked for hours cutting boards I didn't nail into place and stacking lumber in piles that vanished by the end of the day. I was so far out of the logic of the operation that I didn't realize we were actually building two houses. I had asked Guy one day about the handsome place under construction at the top of the driveway just off the lane, thinking it was a neighbor's house. It had been

216

framed and sheathed and it seemed to be finished except for doors, windows, and siding. "*There?*" Guy asked, trying to get over his disbelief. "That's the gatehouse. You know, the garage."

The trouble was, whenever I was given a real job, I made mistakes. For four days I worked in the basement, blocking the floor joists. The joists were two-by-twelves that ran every fourteen inches the length of the house, and they had to be held in place by blocks of wood. I kept cutting them too long or too short, and finally I gave up on the skill saw and started cutting them by hand. Each time the basement door opened and light streamed in from outside like the light at the end of a long tunnel, I dropped the handsaw and pretended to be using the skill saw. It was a job that should have taken two days, it took me five. And each day I would be numb with cold after the first hour of the dampness seeping into my bones through the soles of my feet, so that by the time I went home I felt waterlogged.

The house was being built, the proof was right there in front of my eyes, and I was there every day for ten hours working without stopping in order to finish the jobs Larry assigned to me, but I was waiting for the kind of purpose and satisfaction I imagined the Italian masons took home each night. There were three of them, whom I thought of as the father, son, and holy grandfather, and I loved watching them build the granite stone wall that was covering the foundation. They arrived each morning in one truck with the youngest man behind the wheel. The old man got out first and walked straight to the large pile of stones, where he stood for a while by himself until the other two men came up behind him. Then, as if he had been dreaming the stones into their shapes in his sleep, he peered down at the pile and pointed slowly to those he believed would fit together to make the section of the wall they were going to work on that day. The younger men, his son and grandson, gathered those stones from the large pile and moved them slowly to the foot of the scaffolding, where they worked until dusk. There were buckets of cement to be hauled up onto the staging as well, and whenever I watched them it seemed like the most brutal work to me, and it made me think how warm and how comfortable my own life had always been. In the first strokes of sunlight each morning I saw their Saint Christopher medallions glistening as the men leaned over their trowels. I wondered what they thought about as they set each stone in place, stone after stone. While they worked they listened to love songs on their tape deck. The license plate on the truck said "Mike & Missey," and I saw Mike drive off each day at noon and return an hour later.

I realized after a while that I was watching Mike so closely because he resembled the fathers of my boyhood. Men I had feared turning into. But what was there to fear? The dull monotony of the work? Losing a woman to a man in a silk tie? Or being married to a woman who would *not* hunger for more than a man who mixed cement? In the days when I was my father's little boy we lived in a typical 1950s neighborhood of identical houses placed side by side, and mothers who came to the door in curlers. Our fathers wore their hair like Pat Boone and hummed big band swing tunes when they did their seasonal chores outside, raking, mowing, painting, shoveling snow. Just home from the war, these men went on to become hourly laborers in steel mills, salesmen on the highways, tradesmen. These were working men before anything else, and so their summer vacations, their new cars, their babies, and their remodeled attics and basements — all that amounted to a real life, was made possible by holding down a job. They took their jobs for life and no one talked about stress or domestic violence or alcoholism. Of course it must have been there, across the street, next door, down the hallway, but that was a time when you concealed your misery rather than sell it to Oprah as entertainment. The fathers of my boyhood had remained in my memory as weary men who drank beer in their white T-shirts after work, their muscles glistening.

Watching Mike get into his truck one day at noon to drive home for his lunch hour I remembered my best friend's father at the end of Clearspring Road; every summer Mr. Burke took his two-week vacation on one of the Finger Lakes in upstate New York. Always the same two weeks in August, always the same lake, the same cabin. Like the captain of a ship, he kept a log of each trip, departing the house at precisely the same time each summer, stopping for exactly two hours at the Baseball Hall of Fame in Cooperstown, stopping at the same gas stations and restaurants along the way and only staying as long as he had the previous summer. He was trying to beat the time he had made the summer before, eight summers before, trying to better the miles per gallon. I remembered his son telling me this in the sixth grade one day after school when we stopped on the way home to throw rocks at the steel water tower. The story must have fit some idea I was already holding about these men. Mr. Moyers had a backyard pool (not a real pool that was sunk into the earth but a sheet metal corral resting sadly on the ground), and after someone stole his pool furniture he began blackening his face at night with shoe polish and waiting behind the bushes. Mr. Adelman had a punching bag in his basement and once caught us spying on him there, pounding his fists into the bag for all he was worth while tears streaked down his face. "Get outta here!" he screamed at us. Arthur Crosby's dad had a black-and-white photograph of a tiny

Japanese man tied up in ropes like a ham and being fed to a boa constrictor by a group of GIs on the other side of the world. The man was wearing only his undershorts and you could plainly see the terror on his face. Paula Edmunds's dad smashed a badminton racket across her head after she accidentally broke a garage window. I hated them all and felt certain I was better than them. Smarter, anyway. To me, all of them looked trapped in their ranch houses, their little squares of lawn. *Ranch house* — what could ever have been more unlike a ranch than those pitiful, nailed-together, interchangeable boxes? It was a name thought up by the composers of mass culture to make these men feel like cowboys, like real *individuals,* while they were being homogenized right out of their shoes. Fools. I thought of them as fools. They came on parents' night to our little brick elementary school to tour the fallout shelter and to watch us do our duck-and-cover drills. These were men of such astonishing ignorance that they believed their children would survive a nuclear attack by hiding beneath their classroom desks.

I had no idea why the excavation crew dug an enormous hole six feet deep and eight feet wide that ran the entire length of the foundation wall along the front of the house, but every night the hole filled with water from the marsh and my job was to go down into the hole and turn on the pump as soon as I got to work. One morning I slid down one bank, broke through the ice, and landed in water up to my neck. I started the pump and then headed home for some dry clothes, cutting through the golf course so I wouldn't be seen by the rest of the crew coming to work.

I spent the rest of the day moving boulders in a sleet storm. There were nearly a hundred of them strewn across a quarter acre of land that had to be cleared for drainage pipes, and they were too heavy to lift, so I had to stay down on my knees to push them an inch or two at a time with my thighs. Suddenly it began to snow, the first snowfall of winter, and when I looked up I discovered Mike watching me from his scaffold. I paused and looked down at the next rock. It was like looking at the truth; all my life I had observed men like Mike and written the script for their dull lives, but now I imagined him writing the script for mine, lying in bed tonight with his beautiful wife, maybe drawing on a cigarette that suddenly illuminates her cheek, her breast in the dark room, and then telling her about the old guy pushing rocks with his knees all afternoon. "What a loser, you know? At his age. No skills. Nothin', man."

I thought that maybe he had figured out what I had never known about myself until then. All the judgments I had made about guys like him, the fathers from my boyhood, were built upon an extraordinary arrogance and privilege that came along with the territory of success.

When I got home from work I had dinner with Colleen and the kids, egg noodles and peas. Nell was trying to persuade me that we should let our dog have a litter of pups. I was distracted, way out there, thinking mostly about how I had always tried to please people who I believed to be above me. I was thinking how someone like Mike, a bricklayer, wouldn't have tried to appease the feminists in the English Department at Colgate or anyone else. He wouldn't have spent his energy trying to insinuate himself into another life that looked better, easier. I began thinking again about *Death of a Salesman*. I was trying to remember the end of the play, where they are burying Willy Loman. I was mad at myself for having taken my copy of the play to the dump with the rest of my books, and after dinner I drove into Portland, to the library. I stood in the stacks reading the final pages of the play. There was a homeless man in a ragged brown coat at the far end of the darkened aisle, sitting on the floor with his head bowed. Biff speaks first at his father's grave.

> **Biff:** *There were a lot of nice days. When he'd come home from a trip; or on Sundays, making the stoop; finishing the cellar; putting on the new porch; when he built the extra bathroom; and put up the garage. You know something, Charley, there's more of him in that front stoop than in all the sales he ever made.*
>
> **Charley:** *Yeah. He was a happy man with a batch of cement. . . .*
>
> **Biff:** *He never knew who he was.*
>
> **Charley:** *Nobody dast blame this man. You don't understand: Willy was a salesman. And for a salesman, there is no rock bottom to the life. He don't put a bolt to a nut, he don't tell you the law or give you medicine. He's a man way out there in the blue, riding on a smile and a shoeshine. And when they start not smiling back — that's an earthquake. And then you get yourself a couple of spots on your hat, and you're finished. . . .*
>
> **Biff:** *Charley, the man didn't know who he was.*

It was plain to me at last. Like so many in my generation I had been a salesman my whole life, selling myself to whoever I thought might make me more of a success. Now, like Willy, I had a couple of spots on my hat.

The next day it snowed again. A real storm fell over the coast of Maine. The masons worked through it, as we all did. I watched Mike walking to his truck at the end of the day. He knew who he was, and like all people who know who they are, a kind of grace attended him and his work. The snow that afternoon cast a silence upon the house, and I felt changed.

15

For three days I had a good job building temporary windows and doors we needed until the custom-made windows and doors arrived from Minnesota. I built them happily from dawn until dusk, recalling how my father and I had done this work together at the start of each winter to block out the wind in the apartments we'd rented when I was growing up. When I nailed the last one in place, the house was closed in and this meant we could begin running propane heaters. That night I fell asleep thinking about working the next day where it was warm.

When I arrived Larry was already there, standing in the hole along the front of the house. He had blueprints spread out on the ground above his head and he had hooked up a second pump, a gas-operated one to augment the electric pump. The motor made it hard to hear what he was saying.

He climbed out of the hole and we knelt down in the frozen

dirt and I tried to follow him as he explained how we were going to build concrete footings the entire length of the hole and then a perimeter retaining wall on top of the footings. He traced his finger along the blueprint. "You can follow it here," he said. "It goes in for twenty-two feet, then it cuts out six feet to grab the front of the porch, then it winds back. See?"

I said I did.

"Let's get going," he said, rolling up the blueprints. "Five days and we'll have it done."

It was work that originally was going to be done in the spring by the excavation crew he had subcontracted. But he'd worried that it would be too wet for too long in the spring and had decided at three o'clock in the morning that we'd do it now ourselves.

We got right into it. Luke lined up the cement truck for two o'clock that afternoon and then he put on his boots and got down in the hole with Larry and me. We measured for the forms, cut the wood, and built them right in the hole and then surveyed them to make sure they were level. All the while the pumps were sucking water that ran in from the marsh. A lot of it was pick and shovel work, and we got soaked and the water froze our clothing. We worked against the clock, cutting the steel rods to reinforce the concrete and laying them in grids in the mud on the bed of the forms. The first day everything went like clockwork. I was fastening the last pieces of steel when the cement truck pulled in at the top of the driveway. We stood in the hole, pushing the cement through the forms with our shovels while it ran down the shute. Then we smoothed out the surface and climbed out of the hole just as it was getting dark.

The next morning we started in again, only this time I was left on my own while Larry and Luke had a breakfast meeting with the architects. It was my first real chance, and I studied the blueprint over and over before I began building the forms. Right from the start, though, nothing looked right. I built one form and then ripped it apart and started again. Then a third time. The blueprints fell into the water and were unreadable and I began to think maybe that would be my excuse. By noon when Larry and Luke returned there wasn't enough time left to finish before the cement arrived. "I'll call and try and stop the truck," Luke said disappointedly.

Larry jumped down into hole. "Let them come," he yelled above the pump.

For a while I tried to keep up with him and be of some help. But then I just stood there. I remembered a moment at the university when pipes had burst in one wall in the conference room of the English department. It was an ancient stone wall and all through the afternoon the room was filled with workmen tearing the place apart with jackhammers and chisels, trying to get to the pipe. Water was running down the hallway, and as a precaution all the utilities had been shut off in the building. The room was dark, the men were shouting and gesturing to one another while the water gushed through the ceiling. It was like a scene from a catastrophe film, and I was standing there watching when one of the professors from the classics department wandered in with a batch of term papers in one hand and said very loudly, "Excuse me, but there's a terrible chill in my office and I wonder what the propects are that heat will be restored this afternoon?" I looked at my colleague standing there in his trenchcoat with all the straps fastened. All of a sudden the workmen stopped and turned and stared at him with that universal and timeless expression that men who work hard reserve for men like college English professors, who don't, the expression that says, *What the fuck planet does this guy live on?*

On the third or fourth day Larry let me cut the steel myself. "Just read the prints carefully," he said. I did, but I still cut twenty pieces each two inches short. "Do them again," he said.

Halfway into the job the temperature fell to fifteen below zero, and every time I bent over in the icy water it felt like my bones were grinding in their sockets. At one point I had to climb out of the hole to piss. I walked around to the back of the house, and when I took out my penis it was covered in wet blood the color of raspberries. I bent over and looked through the open fly. There was blood everywhere, it had soaked my long underwear and my boxer shorts and was half frozen, thick and sticky like jam. It scared me and I jumped around, tearing off my clothes until I found a small cut along a blood vessel.

I had been back in the hole just a few minutes when I looked up and saw a woman standing there smiling at me. "Will you give me a grand tour?" she asked pleasantly. At first I thought I hadn't heard her correctly. I knew she was a Prouts Neck woman because she had one of those highly bred collies with the sawed-off legs with her. "I've known Larry since he was a boy," she said just as pleasantly. "He won't mind if you give me the cook's tour."

As soon as I agreed and showed her inside, her mood changed. "You could build places like this at the turn of the century," she snarled at me. "But today they just scream one word — *Pretentious!* Look at that London stairway," she exclaimed.

"Yeah," I said stupidly.

"How many bathrooms? I heard TEN!"

"It's only eight," I said. "Unless you count the carriage house."

I thought I heard her dog growl at me on the way out. She cut me off at the door and turned back for one last look. "A London stairway," she said disdainfully.

The house was a curiosity, and when the owners of the summer houses returned for long weekends, they often wandered by. "Excuse me," Larry called from the roof when two women emerged from the house. "Who are you?"

They told him that a certain man from Prouts Neck, one of the largest landowners, had given them permission to take a tour. A few minutes later this man appeared, dressed in a camouflage jumpsuit that looked like he had just ordered it from a duck-hunting catalog. "I'm so sorry," he said unctuously, "the last thing I want to do is upset you. What tool is that you're using there?"

Larry sensed at once that the man was trying to appease him. "It's a hammer," he called back to him.

It was so cold those days, so numbingly cold working in the hole, that once when I stopped to smoke my coffee-break cigarette I set fire to my glove without realizing it.

The subcontractors arrived one morning and began unloading the forms we needed to start the retaining wall. The foreman was a goofy-looking guy who stood in one place eating donuts while he yelled orders at his crew. I figured he was the son who had inherited the business. It was barely above zero and the wind was vicious and he kept telling his men to set things down one place and then changing his mind and telling them to move them someplace else.

He was back again the next morning, shouting more orders. The electric pump had gone off for some reason, and I was down on my knees in the water checking to see if it was clogged. I unplugged it and was about to plug it in again when he yelled at me: "Somebody got electrocuted doing the same thing last week. You better smarten up."

I turned and looked at him. All four of his workers had stopped and were looking at him too. And then they turned to me. It was just a moment, but it was worth something to me. I felt like his workers couldn't afford to tell him to shut up, but I could speak for them. I raised the electric cord so he could see it. I held up the plug from the pump so he could see that too. Then I plugged it in and held it in my hands until he turned and walked away. One of his workers shook his head and chuckled to himself. It felt good.

The next day when I got to work Cal was standing there, holding a paper bag. "How you doing?" he asked.

"Digging ditches," I said.

"You'll be strong by spring," he said, handing me the bag.

Inside were a beautiful pair of work boots. Leather with felt liners. "I can't take them," I said.

"You have to," he said.

I was thinking about Cal when I climbed the ladder the next day to paint a coat of primer on the trim at the roofline. It was a long way up, fifty or sixty feet. I was holding on with one hand, carrying a gallon of paint in the other and thinking about how Cal had said that the reason so many people were unhappy these days was because they had lost control of their lives . "I was looking around my house the other day," he told me with dismay, "and I realized that I don't own anything anymore that I can fix myself." At the top of the ladder I stepped onto the plank that hung from wall brackets just below the roof. I started painting, inching my way along the plank. Somehow when I took a half step back I missed the plank. I felt my heel in the air, and a cold emptiness rushed through me. I couldn't move for a long time. I stood there not really thinking about anything but how nice it would be just to drop down to my knees slowly and carefully and then to somehow lie flat on the plank and wrap my arms around it and spend the night there.

It was Rob who finally came outside to look for me. It was quitting time on a Friday afternoon. "Hey," he called up to me. "What are you doing up there?" I told him I couldn't move and he stood at the bottom of the ladder and talked to me until I was down. Inside the locker room everybody took turns telling about when it had happened to them the first time. "I call it the ten-minute heart attack," Rob said, handing me a bottle of beer. When he saw that my hands were still shaking, he opened it for me with the claws of his hammer.

Just before Christmas I was telling a friend about my last day in the hole. Somehow it had fallen to me to prepare the section of earth where the main sewer pipe ran out from the basement wall of the house, through the hole before it was filled in with six feet of gravel and concrete. Everyone else had gone on to do other things, so I cut some shims, triangle-shaped pieces of wood to place under the pipe so that it ran downhill slightly, away from the house. Then I covered the pipe with straw. It took maybe twenty minutes, but it hit me that I had, in my hands, the one job that would sabotage a rich man's house. All I had to do was turn the little shims so that the pipe ran back *toward* the house. My little secret would have been buried beneath gravel and concrete, and no one would have found out until the toilets had been flushed about forty times and the stuff started backing up the drainpipes of the house. "A year ago I think I might have turned it backwards," I said to my friend. "I don't know why, but for a long time after I was fired, I just wanted to take something."

He listened patiently, a good-hearted, hardworking man who had already paid off the mortgage on his house and set aside enough money for his three kids' college education. Then he wrote me a beautiful letter that ended this way: "In doing your work this winter, you will have extracted your own pound of flesh from the rich man who will in legal title own it. But in a true sense, the edifice will always be more yours than his."

The morning I was filling in the hole I heard someone say, "Hey, Professor Snyder, what's up?" I looked up and saw one of my former students standing there. The last time he had seen me I was lecturing about Edgar Allan Poe. We walked home together. He related that he was trying to find work with a nonprofit environmental organization. I told him about the sewer pipe I had buried that day. "I could have ruined the owner's dream," I said.

We kept walking. "Rich asshole, building a goddamned mansion on friggin' wetlands," he said. "You should have screwed him, man."

We had a New Year's party at work. At noon Larry spread pizza and beer across a sheet of exterior plywood set on sawhorses, and he gave everyone a hooded sweatshirt and the rest of the day off with pay. The last thing I did was carry some two-by-eights inside. I was walking along with a stack of them trailing behind me when they suddenly got lighter. I turned and saw Billy's son, President Bush's grandson, grabbing the other end to help me.

When word came that the owner was coming in two days we all wanted everything to be in order, right down to no empty beer bottles in the trash can in the locker room. My job was to clean the place again, not just the job site this time, but all the property that surrounded it. I climbed the owner's tree to get a plastic sandwich bag that had blown into the branches. I crawled through the thickets of his marsh and got one of my boots sucked off trying to reach a Styrofoam coffee cup.

I never saw him. I was in the basement painting trim boards for Luke. I had one bare foot propped up on a roll of insulation next to a propane heater trying to thaw it out, and dried blood caked to my left ear from an infection that was getting worse. Two women in mink coats appeared in an exhaust cloud of perfume. "Have you got anything warm to drink?" one asked. The lady beside her was carrying a Gucci bag stuffed with decorating samples. I told them I was sorry. "If they put fiberglass showers in the bathrooms, the whole house will be ruined," I heard the lady exclaim.

"We've all got blood on our hands," Mark said in the locker room after the owner gave us a dozen donuts for our coffee break and went over blueprints of the kitchen with Larry, who was trying to reassure him that there would be plenty of counter room for his Cuisinart.

"Building a house like this," Mark went on, "so much material, so much waste. So big. We shouldn't be building houses like this anymore. And what kind of guy needs a house this big?"

"It's work through the winter," Rob said.

"I know what it is," Mark said.

Late that afternoon I found a place on the third floor where rain had come in through the roof. There was a half inch of water standing on the floor and the only thing I could think to do with it was scoop it into a bucket with a snow shovel. I worked away at it as if I were bailing a sinking boat, and kept going right past quitting time. I was laughing at myself right through it, and telling myself that the water would have disappeared eventually, but I didn't want to take a chance that the plywood floor would be damaged. I walked all the way home thinking about what I had just done, laughing out loud at times. I decided that I hadn't done it for the owner or for the money; my allegiance was to all the hard work that had gone into laying the floor.

At the end of the second week of January the shingles arrived. Hundreds of boxes of cedar shingles stained gray. I stacked them in the garage, thinking of all the work and of the weeks and weeks of paychecks they represented. A young man from the landscaping crew came into the garage to get out of the wind for a while. He asked me what it was like working for Larry and Billy. He had heard about a painting contractor they wouldn't hire because he didn't pay his workers a decent wage. I knew what he wanted to know. "I get fifteen bucks an hour," I said.

"Unreal," he said, walking away, "nine years and I don't get half that."

Larry started me on the back of the carriage house, the one place that would never be seen. He showed me how he wanted it done, how to run a chalk line and then nail a board along the line to use as a guide, setting each shingle on the edge of the board and moving along, one at a time. Right from the first shingle, I loved the order and the slow momentum of it, and how it steadily amounted to something that looked finished. I loved the heaviness of the hammer in my hand and its solid sound in the cold air.

"I need production," Larry said to me at the end of the first day. We stood together looking at the five rows I had finished. "You have to move a little faster."

I was sure I would. But each day was about the same. Part of the trouble was that it had turned brutally cold. It was below zero when I began each morning, and barely above through most of the day. I dropped five nails for every one I managed to get into place and some days there would still be three hours left to go when I'd look at my watch, thinking I couldn't take the cold another fifteen minutes.

Working up the gabled end of the carriage house was even slower because I had to cut the shingles at the ends of each row to follow the slant of the roofline and to fit tight against the trim that had already been nailed on. I used a knife to cut them and a block plane to finish them. By eleven o'clock one morning, all the subcontractors had gone home and we were waiting to get hit by the first big northeaster of the winter. The ocean was buried beneath sea smoke, the temperature with the wind chill was thirty-seven below. I was high up on a ladder putting the last few shingles in the peak of the gabled end when Larry came around the corner. I saw him standing there. It had just begun to snow. He took the hammer out of his belt and I watched him use the claws to pry up the piece of trim at the end of my rows.

"I cut them all along the angle," I said hopefully.

"Yeah," he said, "but I wanted them to slide *under* the trim. You see, like this? That's the only way to make it watertight."

He started peeling off the shingles with the hammer. It made a horrible noise, the creaking nails and the ripping sound as the shingles snapped and split into pieces that fell into the snow. I was doing the math in my head—fifteen bucks an hour times ten, times the five days I'd wasted. "You'll have to start over on this end," he said. "Don't worry about it."

This happened on a Friday afternoon. I worked alone, on my own time, all day Saturday until I had it done right. Monday I came into the locker room for lunch and I heard Billy saying something to Larry about the labor costs. They stopped talking as soon as I came in, but for the rest of the day I felt it coming, and when Larry told me he was going to lay me off because the doors and windows were late and they had to go in before we could really shingle the place, I didn't believe him.

The next day, without work, I paced from room to room until finally I walked back to the house and volunteered to make the dump run. "I just need something to do," I said.

I spent every day of the next two weeks waiting for Larry to call me back to work and walking down to the beach where I could look down the shore to the house to make sure that the doors and windows weren't in and that no shingles had gone on.

It came down to needing one day's work to put together enough money for our February rent, and when I called Larry to ask him if he needed me to do anything he told me to come in the next morning. I got dressed, then stopped to say goodbye to Colleen. "Wipe off your lips," she said. "You've got Maalox on your lips."

I spent the whole ten hours on my hands and knees picking up every piece of paper and every stick of wood inside and outside the house and the carriage house. I was picking up wood shavings and telling myself that all work had dignity if it paid you enough to make your rent. The guy driving the bulldozer jumped down from the machine and came up to me. "That guy who gave you the boots?" he said. "Cal?"

"Yeah?"

"He died," he said. "I guess he was full of cancer."

It left me feeling helpless again and angry, and at the end of the day I walked the long way home, hoping the kids would be asleep by the time I got there. But when I came in, the three oldest ones were right there telling me that they had driven by with Mommy and seen me at work. "What were you doing crawling in woods?" Erin asked.

Before I had to answer, Cara came into the room crying. She had lost her baby doll outside and she wanted me to go out and look for it. I searched the lane and eventually found the doll, and when I handed it to her she pointed to one foot where a shoe was missing. "You want me to go find the shoe?" I said.

She nodded and I went back outside.

Late that night my father telephoned from Pennsylvania. We had spoken maybe twice since I had screamed "Love it or leave it!" at him the year before. The last time I had seen him, a year before that, he sat me down in front of the television and VCR to show me a tape he had made from a documentary called "Things That Are Not Here Anymore," or something close to that, a nostalgic look at Philadelphia, the "city of brotherly love," in the halcyon days when families could still walk the streets at night without fear. We had argued then as well; my father blamed the permissiveness of the 1960s — rock and roll, pot, coed college dormitories, draft dodgers, and long hair — for the disintegration of the nation he had known as a young man. It was an old, old story; the heroes of his youth — soldiers and presidents — became the villains of mine.

"What can I do to help?" he asked me on the telephone. "When a man loses his job, people have to help out until he gets back on his feet again."

"It's okay," I said, "I have a job. I'm doing carpentry work."

He was relieved. He told me how, in the months before I was born, right up until the day my mother died, he was helping her father build his little house on School Street. He remembered how hot it had been shingling the roof and how he and my grandfather sat on the roof in the late afternoon drinking cold beer. He still remembered how good the beer had tasted, and he told me that everything he ever knew about using tools he had learned helping build that house.

I'd never heard him talk about this before. Suddenly I wished more than anything else that my father was in the room with me and that the two of us could stay up all night talking in front of the fire. I wanted to hear all the stories he had never told me, and I wanted to tell him that he had never deserved to be treated the way I had treated him.

"You were a very good college professor," he said to me. "Someday you'll teach again." Then he went on to tell me that he had taken it upon himself to write letters for me to Colby College and the University of Maine, places where I had once taught.

"I don't understand," I said.

"Well, I wanted to help, that's all. I just made a few phone calls. Every place I called remembered you."

I took some time before I spoke. "They won't forget me now, that's for sure," I told him. "Listen, Dad—you can't do that, all right? I know you want to help, but that's not the kind of help I need. Don't ever do that again, okay?"

I pictured him at the other end of the line, in the tiny apartment in Pennsylvania where he and my stepmother lived. I'd never visited them there but my brother told me about the time he arrived to find their landlord yelling at them for turning the heat up too high. They just stood there, my brother said, and the landlord scolded them like they were little children. The last time I saw my father he had taken a bus to visit us. We spent a lot of the time yelling. When it was time for him to leave I drove him to the bus station and dropped him at the front door. The door was plate glass, as was the whole front of the terminal. In my rearview mirror I watched as he kept trying to get inside through a window until some stranger opened the door for him.

"Well," he said sadly, "I was only—"

"I know, I know," I said.

He had become an old man, and as soon as his voice left the line I began to miss him.

Sometime in the night I decided that I wanted to tell him something or give him something that would bridge the distance between us. I remembered one of his sisters telling me that, as a boy, the thing he wanted most was to be like everyone else. He was from a poor family, living in a rundown rented house with no plumbing. He used to carry his little sister outside to the out-house before bed, and she would make him rattle the broom handle inside the seat to clear away the spiders before he sat her down to pee. His teeth were rotten, and this was a source of embarrassment. He had watched his father sell apples in the street during the Depression, and his mother try to make a whole sup-per, night after night, out of a few baked potatoes that she divided among the six of them. And though other familes seemed to have recovered fully from those awful years, his own had not.

He had wanted so badly just to be the same, and when the war broke out he got his wish. The day after Pearl Harbor my father, a skinny pigeon-toed boy who had never been away from home ran out of gym class in his shorts and enlisted in the army. At boot camp they pulled out all his teeth, uppers one afternoon, bottoms the next morning, and gave him false ones. They gave him his uniform and he felt at once that at last he was the same. He was on the inside of something.

A few days passed, and when Larry didn't call me back to work I went to Pennsylvania to see my father. When I arrived he was sitting in his car with a bewildered look on his face. The trouble was in the gear indicators, the row of little red numbers and letters — P R N D 2 1 — mounted to the steering column. The numbers and letters were still visible, but the little red arrow that moves as you change gears was gone.

"Bastards in Detroit," I muttered.

"No, it's a good old car, he said.

My father had never been any good with his hands, and I thought maybe this would be enough, maybe if I could fix his car for him all the bitterness between us would be washed away. I crawled down below the dashboard and saw the four screws that held the plastic panel in place. I found where the box holding the gear indicators fastened onto the steering column. "This looks pretty simple," I said. He had had a basement workbench when I was a small boy, and like all fathers in his generation he had kept extra nails and screws in Gerber baby food jars secured to a rack by their lids, but he was hopeless with tools. I started with a flat-head and a Phillips screwdriver, but hours later every tool he owned was in the car and the flashlight that my father was aiming from the passenger side of the front seat was growing dim.

"What time is it?" I asked him.

"It's almost eleven o'clock," he said.

"What time do you go to bed?" I asked.

"Oh, it doesn't matter."

No place to go in the morning, I thought. I knew *that* story.

"I've owned some good Fords," my father said happily. "I think Fords are good cars."

"Yeah, well, this is a Chevrolet," I reminded him. He wasn't listening to me.

"Pop Pop's first car was a Ford. Model-A. Your grandmother used all the money she'd saved from taking in laundry to help him buy it. She was so determined to have that car. She was a woman with a lot of determination, and I can see now that during the Depression, when things were bad, she was the one who kept us all happy."

I said, "I don't remember her as a determined woman at all. Old Pop Pop kicked her around all her life."

He started to respond, but then stopped.

"Pass me that roll of fishing line that I gave you," I said to him. I could tell by the silence that my characterization of Nana had hurt his feelings. "Look," I said, "whenever I was around Nana, she always let Pop Pop walk all over her. That's all I meant."

He let this pass. Then he spoke about the first trip they had taken in a car. "Nana had made him promise that we would all go to Harrisburg," he recalled with a faint smile. "It was a long, long trip from Philadelphia in those days. More than a day of driving. I rode in the backseat with my brother, Robert, my twin brother. I remember Nana telling the two of us that we were going to find her sister, Alice, in Harrisburg. An aunt we never knew we had."

He told me that Nana had remained in the orphanage for five years after her sister was adopted and taken away. "All she was ever told was that Alice had been taken to live with a family in Harrisburg. That was all, and by the time we set out in the Model-A for Harrisburg, it had been at least fifteen years since Nana had seen her. Dad thought it was a stupid idea, but Nana was determined to go.

"My brother, Robert, got sick on the way. I remember he got a high fever and Nana held him most of the trip. When we got to Harrisburg my father said, 'Well, where do you want to go now, Ada?' She had him drive from one neighborhood to another. He drove slowly up and down the streets while she went from door to door. I watched her. The front door of each house would open and the people would shake their heads no. We just kept driving up and down streets and she kept going from door to door, and then she knocked on one door and I saw her fall into someone's arms. Just like that. She had found her sister.

"Robert got worse on the way home. Three days later he went into a coma and died. So Nana lost a son and found a sister in three days' time."

I looked up at his face and I could almost see him as a small boy in the backseat of his father's new car watching his mother go from door to door in a faraway city until she found her lost sister's embrace.

The next morning we stood bleary-eyed in front of the television, getting our fix of news to jump-start us into the day. On the screen were pictures of a huge building that the news reporter called the "White House," and it was surrounded by tanks. We stood there half asleep, both of us in our boxer shorts trying like hell to figure out what was going on. It took a while before it was explained that this was an old tape of the Soviet parliament building during the attempted coup led by the group of hard-line Communists in 1991. That had been the end of Communism. I had a feeling watching the tape that America would be next, but for once I kept my mouth shut. In my silence I felt our common ground: here we were, two men, neither young, neither with money, neither earning a penny or holding down a job or owning a house, both thoroughly confused by the way the world was turning.

16

The whole time we had lived at Prouts Neck, whenever Colleen asked me to go with her on the cliff walk I had an excuse. And then finally she gave up asking.

When I got home from visiting my father I asked her if we could take the walk together. It was early morning and when we started out I told her everything my father had said. Hiking past the big houses, I pointed out the copper flashing and window casements, the way the trim caught the edges of the shingles. Little things I had learned from the job. "I'd like to build a house for you some day," I told her.

"That would be nice," she said.

The sun was bright and red, and it hung just above the roof of the big summer hotel.

"It's so cold," Colleen said. "I don't know how you can stand working outside in this cold."

I took her hand. I was going to tell her how I missed the cold work and how good it had felt to be earning our way again, and how I was worried that Larry wouldn't call me back to work and that once the house was finished I wouldn't be able to find more work. I wanted to tell her all these things, but I was suddenly so tired of talking about myself that I just kept silent as we walked along the beach.

Suddenly Colleen stopped and put her arms around me. "I'm cold," she said.

I reminded her that when we had first started dating, whenever she was cold I would ask her to dance, looking for an excuse to put my arms around her.

"So," I said, "do you want to dance?"

"There's no music," she said coyly. "And you hate to dance."

She looked at me. "I'm sorry as hell about everything that's happened," I told her. "That last year at Colgate I applied for twenty-three jobs. Six more our first summer back in Maine. Thirty-four last year before I went down for the count. Another thirty-three this fall. I tried, Colleen, but I guess it's pretty clear, I'm not going to be a professor again."

After a moment she said, "Maybe not."

"Dance with me anyway," I said.

I hummed "Moon River" and pretended to trip over her feet, and then I just held her close.

Larry was true to his word. He called me back to work the day the windows arrived. We had to get all seventy-nine of them in place in advance of a blizzard that was blowing up the coast. The sky was black when I walked down the shore. Out at sea there were ships heading into the cove, their running lights like low-hanging stars. We worked without a break, and I was on the south end of the house when the Italians finished the chimney just as the snow

243

began to blow across the marsh. It was a beautiful stone chimney, and they stood there for a moment looking up at it, blocking the snow out of their eyes. I told the old man that it was something, and I stood next to him, waiting for him to mark the moment in some way. He took one last look and said, "There it is." Then he turned and picked up his lunch box and walked to his truck.

Eleven hours after we arrived that morning we finished the last window. Larry had cut his face on a nail and there was dried blood on his cheek. He was happy. "Let it snow," he said. "Another month and this place will be close. Real close."

My last job that day was to climb up onto all the scaffolding and turn the planks onto their edge so they wouldn't get buried under snow, and then to bring all the ladders down off the sides of the house. I got all but one plank. It was forty feet above my head and I could barely see it in the blowing snow.

The waves were breaking over the seawall when I began walking home. I was sure the wind was blowing at better than fifty knots. It took me almost an hour to get home. Colleen had taken the kids to her mother's, and I got a fire going and then fell asleep in a chair and dreamed about the snow piling up on that last plank that I hadn't moved. The snow would pile up on the plank and then the weight would snap the plank in half and both pieces would go sailing in the wind, right through the beautiful triple windows.

I put all my clothes back on and started down the beach. I climbed up the scaffolding, tied a length of rope to one end of the plank, and lowered it down into the snow.

Overnight the storm passed and I was the first one at work in the morning. The living room, an eighty-six-foot-long great hall with three Rumford fireplaces, twenty windows, and nine sets of double doors each ten feet tall with eight, one-foot-square panes of glass, was drenched in sunlight. It was more than just the light. The windows and doors made it seem like music had been turned on in the house, and I found myself walking from one room to the next, just looking at the view and imagining people living in this light, pulling a chair up to one window early some morning to watch the ships at sea.

I heard Larry's voice below me, on the stairs. Then Billy saying, "You want what's his name to work with me?"

We worked side by side in silence for a day, just nailing on shingles in the freezing-cold wind. He started at his end of each row, and I started at mine. We met somewhere near the middle, took off the board we were using for a straight edge, raised it another five inches, laid a four-foot level across it, tacked it to the wall, and began the next row. I wouldn't have been able to carry on a conversation anyway, I was concentrating too hard on not making a mistake and on keeping up with him.

The only time Billy spoke was to say, "I have you figured for a Bill Clinton man."

When I asked him why, he said, "Every time I get in my truck after you've taken it to the dump, the radio is on NPR. I like listening to my man, Rush," he said. "Rush isn't on public radio."

I didn't think he wanted an answer so I just kept working. All day long it got colder and colder. We were both muttering under our breath, swearing at the wind, and we had snot frozen on our cheeks, and I thought Billy was trying as hard to picture me being a college professor as I was trying to picture him on the White House Christmas card.

I think it was the bird that opened things between us. For a whole afternoon Billy kept asking me if I could hear a ringing sound. I couldn't. "There it is again," he would say, stopping suddenly. He finally decided that it was a cellular telephone in one of the subcontractors' trucks parked up on the lane. Then at the end of the day when I was picking up shingles in the snow I found a dead bluebird. It was still warm and I held it up for Billy to see.

"Jesus," he said. "And I thought it was a car phone."

"Maybe it was crying to us for help," I said.

"Jesus," he said again, and we ended up agreeing that this said something about the modern age and what men had become in it.

The last day on the carriage house Billy gave me the chance to put on the final shingles. I was up high on a ladder at the highest point on the construction site, looking out over the rooftop of the main house, all the way out into the shipping lanes, where the boats were inching their way north along the horizon. I saw the last flicker of sunlight in a pane of glass four or five miles away at Higgins Beach. I climbed down the ladder and looked up at the work we had done and I felt lucky. When I picked up my tools I was so excited that I forgot to put my glove back on, and by the time I got to the locker room, my block plane was frozen to the palm of my hand.

That feeling of being lucky stayed with me for the whole month until the job was finished. The colder and more unbearable it got, the more I began to realize I was going to miss it. After I confessed to Billy that my kids thought of me as the trash man at the job, he did the cleanup, and twice I called Colleen and asked her to drive by so I could wave to everyone from up on the ladder, my hammer in my hand.

One morning, working in sunlight, Billy said, "There's nowhere I'd rather be and nothing else I'd rather be doing than this, right here."

I knew what he meant.

There were subcontractors everywhere in those last days. Plumbers, electricians, a security crew wiring the walls with sensors. The heating crew putting in the duct work, the sheetrockers. Everytime I walked through the house I had this image of Colleen giving birth to Jack, when he wasn't coming out right and the doctor summoned help and soon there were people everywhere, working and focused on one thing.

Near the end, Larry put me on the front of the main house, the first part of the house the owner would see when he returned, and I worked at it until the weather got warm, wanting it to be perfect for him and for reasons that had nothing to do with things I'd thought much about before. The last time when I climbed down the scaffolding and looked up, the house was bathed in moonlight. It struck me how beautiful a house it was. Larry came up behind me. "It's amazing," he said, "someone draws a picture of a place and then, suddenly there it is, exactly like the picture." He had lived with this place for almost a year, always unwhole, broken into small pieces. He had made a hundred decisions a day, about the pieces, and lay awake at night wondering if he'd made the right decisions, and if he'd overlooked something. But standing there, looking back at the house, the dream was whole, all the pieces had come together.

If I had known Larry better I would have admitted that throughout the winter I had resented the man who owned this house. Though I knew nothing about him, I had thought of him as a luckier man than I was, a man with proof that his life was adding up to something. I would have also told Larry that up until this winter I'd always believed that there would be a slot for me at the top, far from guys with mud on their faces, and I had really always thought I was a little better than these guys and entitled to a life that was more celebrated and easier, a life that eventually reached a point where the struggle to make ends meet subsided.

We said goodbye. Larry was hurrying to finish a toy stove he was building for a daughter's birthday party. He had misplaced his screwdriver and was improvising, screwing the hinges on the oven door with a chisel. I thanked him for the work. "Hey," he said, shaking my hand, "thanks for all your help."

17

I was out of work only a few days when Colleen met a woman who needed her house painted. I went by and looked at the place and gave her an estimate based on the same wage Larry had paid me. I had no idea that most painters charged twenty dollars an hour. My bid was by far the lowest and I got the job. I promised her that because I only took on one job at a time I would work steadily on her house until it was completely finished.

I worked carefully on the place, not simply scraping off the old paint that was loose but sanding and burning off all the old paint, taking it right down to the natural wood. I figured out early on that it took no special skills to paint a house better than anyone else on earth would paint it. It took time, and I had a lot of time. Then, before I said the job was finished, I washed all the windows inside and out, storm windows too.

Word got around and I had a choice of which house I would paint next. I found the work restful; there was a steady cadence to it that seemed blessedly to carry over to the rest of my life. I was able to sleep again without sleeping pills and to eat a meal without indigestion. Best of all I found that I could hold my kids without feeling that I had cast them into darkness, and I could look at my wife without feeling that she would be better off with another man.

I missed the camaraderie of Larry's crew, and because I always took my fifteen-minute coffee break at nine in the morning, as we had at the big house, I thought of them taking theirs. And on Friday afternoon at quitting time I drank a bottle of beer, popping off the top with the claws of my hammer.

I'll never forget the time I ran into a toy store on the way home from work wearing my paint-spattered clothes and the sales clerk looked at me when I handed him a check and said, "You must be a painter." I guess because they were words I never expected anyone to say to me, I thought they were meant for someone else. Then I looked down at the paint on my hands and said with great satisfaction, "Yeah, I am."

Later, when I thought about that moment and why I had felt so satisfied, I realized that it was because of what else I could say now — I'm just a man who paints houses for a living, and who pays his own way through this world, and who takes care of his family and fears for his children's future and doesn't try to become something else and doesn't judge others, and who lays down his tax money willingly because he can afford to help people who can't find their own way. And I'm a man who doesn't expect anyone else to give him a job or security or a future. I work for myself, and I'm a man who is going to become good enough at working with his hands that someday he is going to build a house for his family. And if I'm lucky, someday I'm going to spend more time with my friends.

I felt all of that, the meaning of it had settled deep inside me.

We had to move out of the cottage on Memorial Day, so we headed way up the coast to be near friends from Bangor. There was a beautiful house just a few hundred yards from Frenchman Bay at a place called Hancock Point, and soon we were living there in exchange for painting the place for the woman who owned it. She had just lost her husband to cancer and was so grateful for my work that I began fixing little things that needed repair: a screen door, floorboards on the front porch. Before long I spent a little money on some tools, all the tools that I had learned to use while working for Larry, and took on other work. Three weeks ripping off the clapboards on the back of a house, taking off the sheathing beneath the clapboards, cutting out rotten sills, replacing them and the exterior wood, and then painting it all. Expert carpenters earn around twenty-five dollars an hour in Maine and usually take a long time getting through all the work they take on. I discovered that I could charge fifteen dollars an hour, plus the cost of materials, and show up when I said I would show up, and finish the job, clean up after myself, and move on. Under these conditions there was plenty of work.

God, were we happy. There was an apple orchard in the back-yard and a beautiful porch in front where we sat listening to the bell buoy tolling in the harbor and to the beautiful white-throated sparrows singing from the tops of the tall cedar trees. The oldest girls went off each morning to the village green, where they picked up the mail and stopped for library books and planned their social schedule with a couple of dozen other little girls on the Point. I couldn't remember ever having been happier. Colleen spent her days picking wild berries with the kids, or searching the shore for beautiful bits of sea glass that washed in like jewels from old shipwrecks. In the evenings we read to each other and ate popcorn out on the porch, where we could look up and see the headlights of cars going up and down Cadillac Mountain like stars moving across the sky. There were five bedrooms in the house, but we all slept in the big front room, where we played a game with the cars on the main road, guessing how many would go by before we fell asleep. There was enough sunlight to work thirteen-hour days and I will always remember coming home at dusk and hanging my carpenter's belt over the railing of the porch where Colleen had everyone waiting for me, the kids in their pajamas and her hair in braids the way she had worn it when we first met.

Of all things, we became sailors at Hancock Point. I fixed up an old wooden boat I had bought for practically nothing, and the first day I was sailing her in the bay a boat historian spotted me and told me the boat had been built for Charles Lindbergh and was worth a good bit of money. I sold her to a museum in Massachusetts and used the profit to get us a boat heavy enough to take us out to the far reaches of the bay, where one morning a whale came up half a football field off our bow.

We sailed every morning before I went off to work, and throughout the summer our friends and my former students visited. We had unhurried picnic suppers on a blanket in the apple orchard. I would often just lean back and look at all the happy faces. They were matchless summer days like none that I had ever had before.

In the fall we moved back to the cottage at Prouts Neck and the kids took the same school bus to the same school they'd gone to the year before, thus fulfilling my promise to Nell that she would not have to leave her friends again. Larry had recommended me to the owners of the mansion I had helped build, and I was hired to be caretaker. This gave me the chance to have a set of keys and to show the place to friends when they came to visit. I never opened the door and stepped inside without feeling a sense of wonder and also pride.

I took on a big house-painting job that carried me right up to the start of cold weather. I repaired a foundation and replaced the basement windows on another house with double-paned custom windows that I built out of hardwood in my garage for exactly half what the flimsy ones made of pine sold for in the big discount store.

It was all good work that paid me a living wage, a wage that enabled us to raise a family without the wild and demeaning acrobatics that most parents are required to perform if they both hold down jobs.

After all the difficulties of the past few years I wanted to do something special with Colleen, something romantic. I was up on the ridgeline of a roof one day, repointing a chimney, when the sound of a far-off train whistle made me turn my head. Colleen was far too practical to endorse the idea publicly, but I could see in her eyes a momentary flash of delight and excitement when I told her I wanted to take her on a long train trip, just the two of us.

The same look was in her eyes when we boarded the Lake Shore Limited in Boston's South Station a few weeks later and an old porter named Ludy showed us to our room. We were on an overnight run to Chicago, traveling first class all the way to California and back, the first time we had left the kids in ten years.

"Is that so?" Ludy said when I told him that the last time we had slept on a train was after we eloped in England and rode trains all the way to Austria. He lit a little lamp in the closet and showed us the special footlocker for our shoes.

"This is beautiful," Colleen said to him.

"Oh, it sure is, ma'am," he replied, "as long as you got a lot of time or a lot of money it's a fine way to travel."

"We're spending the last of our money," she told him. "We thought it was worth it."

He smiled at her and said, "Sometimes that's what a person *has* to do, get up and ride on a train no matter what."

She showed him photographs of the kids. I hadn't known she had brought these, and she was surprised when I showed her that I had brought my own: four pictures, one of her with each baby in the delivery room, minutes after she gave birth. We looked at them carefully, telling each other what we remembered, both of us amazed at the details we had forgotten.

We fell asleep in each other's arms. Sometime in the night I got up and smoked a cigarette in the space between cars where cold air blew up from the tracks. I felt like we were doing the right thing. I thought about our honeymoon on trains. The "Night Rider" from London's Victoria Station to Scotland. The old upholstered seats and wooden doors. The station somewhere in the Alps where we got off to mail postcards home, announcing that we were married.

Outside our window there were factories on the landscape, shapeless buildings blackened with soot and surrounded by high fences that went on forever. I thought of the night-shift laborers.

I pictured them getting out of their beds in dark rooms, moving slowly and trying not to wake anyone. I knew what they might feel like.

We had some time to kill in Chicago, and we had arranged to meet another former student at the station. From where we were sitting around a little table I could see a newspaper stand where customers were lined up to buy lottery tickets. There were men back behind the stand reading the skin magazines. "That's America," I said.

"So is *that*," Colleen said, gesturing to a white-haired old man she had been watching in the next booth. He was reading Proust one word at a time with a magnifying glass.

We were like children in the little room where everything folded into the walls. We crossed the farmlands of Illinois talking about a new plan for Colleen to go to graduate school so she could have a career. It sounded wonderful to me. We spoke about how we would take the kids on this trip one day and how they would love the train. Just speaking of them set off a long conversation about each child. When we returned home Erin would be auditioning for a part in a professional children's theater, and she was terribly excited about this. She was ten years old and now could hear the hum of the culture in the distance. I thought that lately she had begun to suspect that it might be humming for her. We agreed that Nell needed to find one thing to take her away from herself. She was a pure athlete, swift and agile, but she had no interest in sports. Colleen was hoping to find someone who had a piano they didn't want. "It's either that or a litter of puppies," she said.

Jack and Cara were still small enough that we had no worries about them; these were the easy years.

I held up the photograph of Cara taken the first time Colleen placed her nipple to her lips. "All husbands should start their days looking at those old pictures," I said.

"Where are we now?" we kept asking one another.

I saw Colleen's face beginning to fill out, softening with rest, looking as it used to look before our struggles began. Along the tracks, there were railroad workers, bundled up in the frozen mornings. I knew what it was like to do such hard work in the bitter cold. If you worked with good people and were paid a living wage, at the end of the day you felt sore and tired and satisfied.

It was snowing in the mountain passes of the Rockies. I thought of my father traveling across these mountains when he was eighteen years old, newly enlisted in the army, away from his mother for the first time, skating across the country that seemed so vast and so dark at night. Coming upon little towns now and then, gas stations and furniture stores, neon lights with letters missing along the way. I thought of his fear, heading into what was unknown. All he had been told was that he would be in the invasion of Japan.

I felt grateful. I climbed up into Colleen's bed and for reasons beyond me it was like crossing the uncertain space that divides one person from another. She was warm in her long underwear and slippers. I remembered our first date, and how we overheard the ladies at the next table talking about Colleen. "Every man wants to marry an Irish girl because they have the most beautiful babies," one of them said.

Early one morning I heard a scream from the car ahead of ours. I ran forward and came upon a woman weeping, leaning against one porter who was trying to hand her a linen napkin to dry her tears while another was on his knees, straddling a fallen man, pushing on his chest and saying, "Come on, Mr. Charles, come on." Then he looked up at the woman and said, "No pulse."

It was a heart attack, and the train stopped at the next town so the body could be taken off. I stood in the vestibule between the dining car and the first class sleepers, watching the conductor and four porters carry the dead man. What came into my head was Willy Loman's eulogy for the dead salesman in Miller's play, and I said the words below my breath: ". . . and by the way he died the death of a salesman, in his green velvet slippers in the smoker of the New York, New Haven and Hartford, going into Boston — when he died, things were sad on a lot of trains for months after that."

A distant relative of ours was working as a painter on the Paramount Pictures lot and he got us a pass to enter at the Melrose gate. It was Colleen's day; I took pictures of her standing in front of a glass case where there were Oscars on display. She put on her best pose in front of a large photograph of Lucille Ball, reruns of whose old shows were the only television Colleen let the kids stay up late and watch with her.

Returning home on the California Zephyr out of San Francisco, Colleen told me one night over dinner that she had known each time I had made her pregnant. "It was one of my secrets," she said as she touched the petals of a rose in the crystal vase.

"You never told me that," I said to her.

She didn't say anything for a while. The waiter brought us peach pie for dessert, and after he left our table Colleen described the place and the time of day or night when each of our children was conceived.

She stopped abruptly after the fourth, and I leaned toward her and said that I knew it was my fault she had lost the baby; I had filled our house and our life with so much fear that it had scared her baby right out of its fragile existence. "I'm sorry," I told her.

She looked up at me and asked if I remembered what we had talked about on the beach the first day we met. I couldn't, and she described an old dream I'd once had of opening a college for the elderly. Old people would pack up and head off to college like eighteen-year-olds. They would live in dormitories and fall in love as if they were freshmen again. Only this time they would study for the sake of learning.

We talked about this idea all the way home. It took three nights to get back. What I'll remember from that journey is that every time I woke up, Colleen was awake, looking out the window, and when I asked her once what was wrong, she said nothing was, she was just too happy to sleep.

The next week I was working in South Portland building shelves for someone's kitchen when Colleen found out about a group of men who played hockey on Saturday and Sunday and needed a goalie. I took Jack with me the first time. It was an outdoor rink and it was seven below zero when the game started. Right away I picked out a tall guy with graceful, long strides and a hard shot as one of the best skaters out there. We'd played maybe forty minutes when he went down. No one actually saw him fall and so we were afraid to roll him over, thinking it might be a head or a neck injury. Someone went to the warming shed to call the ambulance and the rest of us stood around the man and piled our jerseys on him to keep him warm. Jack and I were two feet from him when I heard the death rattle in his last two breaths.

The ambulance drove off without its siren on. The next day his obituary said he was thirty-eight years old and the father of two small children.

Something like that shows you again how quickly life rolls

past. It inspired me to build a skating rink in our driveway, the first I had built since I lost my teaching job. It took me half a day and I got the kids involved so that they were waiting with the same eagerness I felt for the water to freeze and to lace up their skates for the first time. We collaborated as well on the goalie, who we made out of lobster buoys that had washed onto the shore. When the temperature fell below zero I stayed up all night, going outside every hour to put more water on the rink and to admire it. I stood in the moonlight and said to the dog, "Some men are making money, I'm making ice." Nothing else that I had done in a long long time could match its perfection and our first night on the ice I felt like something valuable had been returned to me. The kids went zooming by, the dog's legs flying out from under her as she chased them. Colleen and I goofed around under a full moon and stars so bright and finely cut that they looked as if you could break them like crystal glasses.

The girls got mad at Jack and me for our "fake fighting," so it was just the two of us on the ice after a while. We lay on our backs looking up at the stars when I told him I loved him better than anything. "I love you too, Daddy," he said. "And you see that star right *there?* When you die, Daddy, wait for me on that star, okay?"

Before we came inside he got down on one knee and I used his hockey stick for a sword and knighted him Prince Jack of Scarborough Beach. He would not remember this, but as long as I did, it would hold its own place in the vastness of time, in the paths of stars and streams.

I had steady work right through the winter, and by spring I no longer thought of being a college professor. I just concentrated on the work in front of me. All my life I had thought that if you worked hard you would be rewarded. If you worked your ass off, there would be some reward for you. But now I knew that the reward was just *the chance* to work your ass off.

On school vacation week I took Jack to work with me trying to repair a leaking roof on an ancient house in Cape Elizabeth owned by an eighty-year-old man who lived alone. It was one of those *real Maine houses* that looks from the street like it was the sight of a great and sustained struggle across the years. The trouble was where the shed roof joined the main roof, and Jack and I were up there for five hours, and the whole time the old man sat in his backyard talking to the birds that were drawn there by dozens of homemade bird feeders strung along the length of his clothesline. Jack was seven now and had begun to ask me meaningful questions about why I had been fired from Colgate. The whole time we worked on the roof I was talking to him about his sister, Erin, who had recently taken it upon herself to try and save her fifth-grade teacher's career. A thoughtful young man who painted and lived the solitary life of an artist, he had to leave the classroom one day when he began to cry. Someone came into the classroom and explained to his students that he had been fired. It surprised me when Erin went to his defense because he had pushed her very hard all year and she had often complained. As soon as she learned that his contract was not going to be renewed she organized a petition among her classmates and their parents, and after she collected sixty-two signatures she wrote a letter to the superintendent requesting a meeting with him. She gave me the letter to mail for her one morning as I was going out the door. I confess that I hesitated. I was in the parking lot at the post office in Scarborough, holding her letter and thinking that someday Colleen was going to be applying to this same superintendent for a teaching job, a job that would carry health insurance and full benefits. But in the end I knew that I owed it to Erin to mail her letter. "Maybe your sister will turn out to be a real boat rocker," I called to Jack. He was fiddling with the channel dial on the radio we had set up on the roof, taking his time to find a good station. He knew my rules about the kind of music a man plays when he's high up off the ground and a little scared, maybe, but denying it. Songs by one singer that were originally recorded by another singer are worse than swarming wasps. Anybody singing Beatles songs especially. And Michael Bolton doing his fraudulent version of "When a Man Loves a Woman" could be fatal. Jack didn't want to talk about his sister. He had been after me lately to come up with a brother for him to replace his buddy, Brian Murphy.

"Mom said she won't have any more babies," he said grimly.

"When did she tell you that?"

"In the car."

"When?"

"I don't know. She said we don't have any money."

"We've got plenty of money."

"That's not what she said. She said if we ever got some money she would adopt a brother for me."

"That's a good idea, don't you think?"

"Why do you need money to adopt a brother?"

"I don't know. Maybe you don't."

It turned out that the old man didn't have any money either, and all the way back to Scarborough I kept looking over at Jack. He had his head down most of the way. One of the old man's bird feeders was between us on the seat.

"You don't take an old man's money," I said sternly.

"But we need the money."

"Well, he gave us a bird feeder, so that's one less thing we have to buy. And it was all he had to give us. Besides, it's special."

"No it's not," he said. "It's dumb."

I began a job on another summer house the next week. I met the owner standing outside watching a landscaping crew roll down his new lawn. It was some kind of special grass, he told me, a mixture of Hawaiian grass and Kentucky bluegrass.

He took me inside the house. The walls had all been stripped down to the bare studs. He explained that he was winterizing the place and he took me to the top floor and pulled one of those folding staircases out of the ceiling and we climbed up to the attic. There was no electricity; the only light was seeping up from below, and it outlined the rafters like the ribs on a large wooden boat. He told me he wanted six inches of insulation between the rafters and a plywood floor on top. I knew what this meant; twenty or thirty hours bent over like a monkey inhaling fiberglass. And that was after the hard work of lugging forty sheets of four-by-eight plywood up four flights of stairs.

"Yeah," I told him when we were back outside, "I'll do it."

"I want it done by Memorial weekend," he said.

"I can start tomorrow."

"How much do you charge an hour?"

"Fifteen dollars," I said right away.

He threw his head back and laughed, not really at me, I don't think, but at the idea of paying fifteen bucks an hour. "I could only pay half that," he said.

"I see," I said. I told him the problem was that I needed fifteen dollars an hour to pay our bills each week. He put on his aviator sunglasses and shrugged his shoulders.

I stood there for a few seconds reading the logo on his bright red golf sweater, and then I said, "It's hard work. Monkey work, really. I won't work for less than a living wage when I'm working for rich people."

He sort of smiled at this. Then he said, "Hey, you're entitled to your ideas. It's a free country."

I went home and had supper, and when Colleen and I were doing the dishes she asked me if Jack and I had been talking about adopting a brother for him. She smiled and said that he had come up to her and told her that we didn't need money to have a brother, all we needed was a little bed next to his and some food. "He said all he wants is somebody who understands American so he can read *The Hardy Boys* to him until he falls asleep at night like Daddy does to him."

I ended up going back and telling the man I would do the work for seven fifty an hour. "I need the money," I said.

"Great," he said. He gave me his hand to shake as if no other words had passed between us.

It was brutal work. I wouldn't let Jack upstairs while I put down the insulation. There were no windows in the attic, no ventilation at all. The floor joists were twenty-two inches apart and I had to straddle them on my kneecaps for six hours while I laid in the insulation. Whenever I raised my head an inch too high I got a roofing nail in the back of my skull. If I slid off a joist I would have fallen through to the next floor. On top of this, the four-by-eight sheets of half-inch plywood were too large to get up the narrow stairs so I ripped them all in half first outside, which took three hours that I hadn't planned on spending.

When the sun went down I had to hook up a light so I could see what I was doing. Colleen brought the kids by to say good night to me. Jack was crawling along the section of the floor that I had just nailed down. "Hey," he said, "I can see right through into his closet."

"Let me guess," I said. "Tennis rackets and golf clubs."

"And balls too. Tons of them, Daddy."

I slid over and looked down with him. There were tennis sneakers wrapped in plastic, and there was a beautiful windbreaker with an Olympic emblem on the front and golden threads that wrote the name of his company just above "Proud Sponsor of the 1996 Olympic Games."

"Do you wish I was him?" I asked Jack.

"Nope," he said. "But I wish I was you."

"No, you don't, buddy."

"Yes, I do."

"Why?"

"Because you've got blood all over your face," he said.

He wouldn't go home to bed, he wanted to stay until I was finished for the night. When I got to the part of the floor that was above the man's king-size bed I climbed down and laid a sheet of plastic over it so it wouldn't get covered with fiberglass insulation. "That would be the end of a good night's sleep on that mattress," I said.

"So?" Jack said.

I looked at him. "Well, we don't want to do that to the man's bed."

"Why not?"

"Oh, Jack," I said. "Just because we wouldn't want anyone to do it to us, I guess."

He shrugged this off.

"And it's the work, Jack," I said. "You do the work the right way even if you're working for a jerk." I stopped and blew my nose on my shirttail. Black globs of fiberglass came out. "And don't ever blow your nose on your shirt, okay?" I said with a smile.

The last night on the job all the kids were with me. Nell was practicing her Valley girl talk and Jack was collecting ants in a glass jar. I was putting in the last nails when, like a miracle, it began to rain. It was such a beautiful sound, like buttons pouring from a jar. We lay back on the floor I had built and listened for a long time.

The rich man came to pay me before he headed back to his year-round house. I had thirty-five hours at $7.50 an hour — $262.50. I didn't invite him inside. He stood on the porch and I stood in the threshold as he wrote out the check.

"You did a great job," he said. "I think I want to put up a ceiling too."

"In the attic?"

"Yes. Would you be interested? I'd pay you the fifteen dollars an hour."

I looked into his eyes. The kids were behind me in the mudroom, getting ready for the school bus. "A ceiling would be harder," I told him. "Holding everything over my head and not being able to stand up straight. I'll do it for eighteen an hour."

"All right," he said.